Praise for *Reinventing Retail*

'Reinventing Retail *is THE wake-up call that t*~~...~~
needs. The message is clear – if c~~...~~
they have to design every part o~~...~~
customer in mind, they will die. F~~...~~
be that way – Ian offers a definiti~~...~~
and insight that can help retailers ~~......~~ *...ese*
turbulent times.'

**Dr Geraint Evans, award-winning CMO,
academic researcher and writer**

'*Ian Shepherd combines a far-sighted analysis of the changing
commercial landscape with a practical set of options for
today's retailers. Not just an essential read, but an invigorating
toolbox of solutions.'*

**Philip Downer, Managing Director,
Calliope Gifts; former CEO, Borders UK**

'*Ian brings decades of experience in customer strategy to this
book.'*

**Clare Iles, Independent CRM and
Customer Engagement expert**

'*Don't want to end up as a footnote in retail history? Then you
have to understand how to operate in the "new normal". Ian
Shepherd's solution is to cut through changes in technology,
consumption, markets and customers to build agile and
responsive organisations that do not just survive, but thrive.
An easy-to-read blueprint that helps retailers capitalise on
strengths and avoid being trapped by weaknesses - it helps
you think through strategy and then supports you in execution.
A must-have for anyone in retail who wants to do more than
just survive in today's volatile market - use this and you should
be able to work out how to thrive.'*

**Professor Christopher Bones, Dean Emeritus,
Henley Business School; Professor Emeritus,
Alliance Manchester Business School;
Chairman, Good Growth**

'Richly populated with "the" answers. Each of which is uncovered at a perfect pace that allows the reader to both take in new ideas and consider the many ways their strategic development will benefit from applying them.'

Richard Hammond, best-selling author,
***Smart Retail**; co-founder, Uncrowd*

Reinventing Retail

Pearson

At Pearson, we have a simple mission: to help people make more of their lives through learning.

We combine innovative learning technology with trusted content and educational expertise to provide engaging and effective learning experiences that serve people wherever and whenever they are learning.

From classroom to boardroom, our curriculum materials, digital learning tools and testing programmes help to educate millions of people worldwide – more than any other private enterprise.

Every day our work helps learning flourish, and wherever learning flourishes, so do people.

To learn more, please visit us at **www.pearson.com/uk**

Reinventing Retail

The new rules that drive sales and grow profits

Ian Shepherd

Pearson

Harlow, England • London • New York • Boston • San Francisco • Toronto • Sydney
Dubai • Singapore • Hong Kong • Tokyo • Seoul • Taipei • New Delhi
Cape Town • São Paulo • Mexico City • Madrid • Amsterdam • Munich • Paris • Milan

PEARSON EDUCATION LIMITED
KAO Two
KAO Park
Harlow CM17 9SR
United Kingdom
Tel: +44 (0)1279 623623
Web: www.pearson.com/uk

First edition published 2019 (print and electronic)
© Pearson Education Limited 2019 (print and electronic)

ISBN: 978-1-292-27077-7 (print)
        978-1-292-27078-4 (PDF)
        978-1-292-27079-1 (ePub)

British Library Cataloguing-in-Publication Data
A catalogue record for the print edition is available from the British Library

Library of Congress Cataloging-in-Publication Data
A catalog record for the print edition is available from the Library of Congress

10 9 8 7 6 5 4 3 2 1
23 22 21 20 19

Cover design by Two Associates

Print edition typeset in 9.5/13, ITC Giovanni Std by SPi Global
Printed by Ashford Colour Press Ltd, Gosport

NOTE THAT ANY PAGE CROSS REFERENCES REFER TO THE PRINT EDITION

To Bridget

Contents

About the author **xi**

Acknowledgements **xii**

Introduction **xiii**

Part 1   The rules of the New Normal   **1**

1   Rule 1: Someone is going to sell your product at cost or less   **3**

2   Rule 2: Everyone knows everything – nothing is a secret   **33**

3   Rule 3: Reputation will make or break a business   **55**

4   Rule 4: Location matters, but for different reasons than it used to   **77**

5   Rule 5: Knowing your customer is key – flying blind won't end well   **97**

6   Rule 6: If a product or process can be dis-intermediated or simplified, it will be   **115**

Part 2 A business plan for the New Normal **129**

7 Building your plan **131**

8 You get what you measure **147**

9 Building your digital skills **163**

10 Getting things moving **175**

11 Taking people with you **189**

In conclusion **203**

Index **207**

Publisher's acknowledgements

86 Luzac & Company: Sun Tzǔ on the Art of War: The Oldest Military Treatise in the World, Luzac & Company, 1910

About the author

Over the last 25 years, Ian Shepherd has served as Chief Operating Officer of Odeon (Europe's largest cinema business), CEO of Game Group (a pan-European retailer with over 1300 stores) and has held senior commercial and retail leadership roles for world-leading brands including Vodafone and Sky TV. Over that period, he has seen the seismic shift from 'analogue to digital' in multiple industries along with the changes in consumer behaviour that followed.

Ever curious about the changing business landscape, Ian has also worked with start-ups, entrepreneurs and innovators and has hands-on experience with the emerging disciplines of data science, customer analytics and with the technologies that power digital retailing.

It is this unusual combination of the experience of leading billion-pound consumer businesses married to a practical understanding of new technologies that is at the heart of the vision for the future of retail outlined in Reinventing Retail.

Ian lives in Oxfordshire, in the UK, with his wife and family and can often be found on twitter (@ianashepherd), and on LinkedIn.

Acknowledgements

I'm lucky to have been able to learn from a lot of brilliant people over my career and much of their wisdom and insight is reflected in the examples and anecdotes throughout this book. I'm indebted to the people I've worked with in consumer and retail businesses and to leaders of other businesses I've shared war stories with along the way. In that context I'd like to offer particular thanks to Justin Linger and his team at Barracuda whose retail networking events have offered a terrific forum for retail leaders to hear from each other.

Thanks are also due to Eloise Cook and her formidable team of colleagues at Pearson for their efforts in helping me turn a set of anecdotes and observations into something I hope resembles a coherent manifesto.

My wife Bridget and my children Jamie and Cara have put up with a lot as I've learned the lessons I share in this book. Retail leadership is important and fascinating but can become all-consuming and take us away from those we love for too long. I am forever grateful for the support and strength my family has offered over the years. Bridget, to whom this book is dedicated, has also offered an incisive economist's perspective on the narrative of this book, and if you find anything in these pages you think is genuinely clever, I probably borrowed it from her.

Introduction

Why now?

This book was born at about 2am one January night in 2012. Stumbling out of the offices of a big London law firm where my team and I had spent the preceding 18 hours negotiating with our own banks over the future of the retail business I ran, I suddenly realised the time, that all the trains and tubes had stopped running and that I was many miles from home.

In the end, we didn't succeed in our negotiations and a UK retail business with thousands of colleagues and operations in nine countries collapsed into administration.

My overriding thought that night, apart from how on earth I was going to get home, was that it should never need to be this way. The cost of a business failing, to suppliers and creditors, to shareholders and lenders but most of all to the people across the business who end up with statutory redundancy pay and no job after years of service is simply too big to be acceptable.

There is an imperative on all of us involved in running retailers to secure them for the future and my team and I had failed to do that. Many of us had joined with optimism about the chances of turnaround, but the reality was that our business had long since been left behind by changing markets and changing customer needs.

As I reflected on that in the small hours of the morning it became important to me to form as clear a view as I possibly could about how we could have avoided getting there in the first place. We'd tried hard (albeit late) to reinvent our business for the new economy – there must be lessons to extract from both our successes and the things we should have done sooner or better.

In the last few years, we've seen plenty of similar business failures – big and long-standing retail brands disappearing from the high street or surviving but in a massively cut-down form. Each example hides a thousand stories like the ones I could tell from my experience – of management teams struggling to find a path through, of board room tensions, of lenders, investors and suppliers showing faith but then in the end showing despair and of that same human cost to the people working across the business.

If you take a long-term economist's view of all of that, and you have no soul at all, then you might be tempted to conclude that it is all part of the tapestry of the free market. Old businesses lose their way, new ones pop up. Technology step changes and evolving consumer needs drive change.

At some macro-economic level that's true, but we make a terrible mistake if we think that that means we should let established retail brands fail without a fight. If there is to be technology change, and if consumer needs evolve, so be it – but there is no fundamental reason why it can't be existing businesses who evolve with them to capture those opportunities. Indeed, it is arguably a better economy where that change happens without the disruption, upheaval and cost of brands disappearing. It is certainly a more humane one.

A new world for retailers

What is driving the turmoil in the retail sector?

Quite simply, the world has changed in the last two decades. A revolution has changed not just the channels consumers can use to make purchases, but also the way they decide what to buy, and from whom.

The key driver of that change is technology. Not only has the internet created a huge, chaotic library of all the information in the world, but revolutions in mobile phone and computer technologies now mean that we have access to that chaos all the time.

This revolution has challenged retailers along with many other consumer-facing businesses. Almost every category of retailing has seen one or more seismic shifts in the rules of the game over this period. New start-ups have threatened and sometimes destroyed long-standing incumbents – a modern business tragedy that has impacted thousands of colleagues and millions of customers.

To equip today's retailers to survive, thrive and grow, it is essential that we understand the ways in which the changed world of the consumer has changed the 'rules of the game' for running a successful consumer-facing business. That is our mission in this book.

Changes in technology have altered consumers' lives in two different ways, each of which has a profound impact on what it takes to be a successful retailer.

The 'first-order' or direct effects of technology change come from how we use it. We can order products online, learn at a distance, explore the world. We can see those first-order changes everywhere – not just in our lives as consumers but in business too, where technology has dramatically extended our horizons from local markets to global and changed almost every aspect of the enterprise from procurement through to billing.

Just as interesting, however, is the 'second-order' impact of technology change. This is what you see when you look beyond how we use technology and start to look instead at how the technology revolution has changed us. We are still biologically the same as our ancestors who lived in caves, but we now have god-like power to influence the world around us. We can fly. We can communicate with others on different continents. We can access vast reservoirs of information. It is understandable if we respond to the changes around us in unpredictable ways, using technology both to educate, protect and enrich ourselves but also to argue, fight and send videos of cats to each other.

Consider the apparently simple task of buying a fridge. Once we'd have had to invest time and energy travelling around from one shop to the next comparing prices and specifications until we either found the best option or got bored and bought the one in front of us. Our choice was limited, not only by our willingness to shop around but also by the products that the retailers we visited happened to have in stock.

Now, not only can we gather all the information we need online, place an order and have our new fridge delivered when we choose, but the second-order impacts of technology change mean that we can read reviews and share opinions from people all around the world. A simple Google search for fridges returns millions of results, including every conceivable product from every possible retailer. In many ways it is easier to buy a fridge now, but the process of choosing one is also more complicated when there is so much information at our fingertips.

The New Normal

These dramatic changes to consumer behaviour are the most important root cause of how the retail world has changed in the last two decades. Businesses now operate in a 'New Normal' – a set of shifts in both society and technology that have forever changed the 'rules of business'.

> **The way brands find customers and grow, the way customers choose what to buy, even the way products are developed and brought to market in the first place are all different now.**

In the everyday normal run of business it can be too easy to focus on the immediate, obvious and literal consequences of the way the world has changed, when increasingly it is the knock-on impacts, the unintended consequences of those changes which both threaten established businesses and create huge new opportunities too.

Let's take e-commerce as an example. One of the most obvious changes of the last 20 years has been the fact that consumers now expect to be able to buy most products and services online – just like our fridge example. That creates some immediate practical challenges for any business:

- build and operate a website which can serve those customer needs
- do business through other, bigger websites which act as virtual shopping malls
- engineer their 'supply chain' so they keep the right amount of stock and have the right delivery options
- integrate all of that, where necessary, with the existing physical store estate to allow returns to store, 'click and collect', etc.

So far, so good. For a decade or more digital strategies have been dominated by this drive to e-commerce and latterly omni-channel retailing of products. Those who were slow to spot the new opportunity gradually died away and those who were nimble survived. New giants of retailing emerged from those companies which started first in the e-commerce sector and captured consumer interest early.

Only now, though, are retailers beginning to wrestle with the knock-on consequences of selling on the internet. The second-order impact of technology change has been to alter how consumers live their lives and change how they decide which brands to buy from and what products to buy. These second-order challenges for your business are:

- If your product can be sold on the internet, how do you compete with dozens of new entrants selling the same products? How can your customers tell the difference between yours and every other competing brand?

- Is there any way to differentiate yourself online other than through lower prices? If not, are we all destined simply to have to sell everything at virtually cost price?

- Even if yours is one of those products which don't sell themselves well online (art, clothes, shoes, highly designed goods), what are the implications of the changes in consumer behaviour for your business?

- How can you take control of the way your brand is formed, discussed and dissected through social media? What do you do about your brand reputation when so many of the traditional marketing channels have changed beyond recognition?

- For retailers with 'traditional' brick and mortar retail outlets, what are those stores now actually for? Are they just expensive display cases? Can they play a role in customer service and therefore in building relationships with valuable customers? Is there a danger that in building your new e-commerce channel you have neglected your stores, leaving them tired and boring?

Those businesses which are really thriving are the ones who are actively thinking about these kinds of fundamental, existential implications of the New Normal. Through this book we'll see world-class retailers finding new ways to connect with customers and making vibrant and entertaining stores the core of a multi-channel offer. Success stories like Hotel Chocolat and Lush in the UK offer rich food for thought for the rest of us.

> **To plot a course for the future, we need to consider how we can best, and most profitably, respond to the new world around us.**

The rules of the New Normal

To understand such a fundamental societal change, we need to break it down into bite-sized chunks – into individual observations or rules that we can use as entry-points to build strategies for our businesses. Here, then, are my rules of the New Normal – rules that were not generally true 20 years ago but are now:

1. Someone is going to sell your product at cost or even less. It might even be you.
2. Everyone knows everything – nothing is a secret and much less information is proprietary.
3. Reputation matters more than it did before and will make or break a business.
4. Location matters, a bit, but for different reasons than it used to.
5. Knowing your customer is key – flying blind won't end well.
6. If a product or process can be dis-intermediated, broken into smaller bits or simplified, it will be.

Over the coming pages, we will dive into each of these rules and come to understand both *why* they are true and also what we can do about them.

Some of the rules are the direct consequences of those first-order changes in technology and society – the growth of the internet, the omnipresence of the smartphone, for example.

Others, however, are the consequences of the evolving needs of consumers in this new world. Faced with more information than we can possibly process, more choices for things to buy and places to buy them than we can ever make we do two extraordinary and apparently contradictory things. First, we embrace the new technology – we search, research and compare products and services in ways we could never have imagined 20 years ago. But second, we revert to the social, community-based creatures that we have always been – we seek reassurance, advice and opinion from those around us, and we embrace the wisdom of the crowd.

This contradictory behaviour is never more apparent than when watching consumers accept the opinions of reviewers of products that they might buy online – just as with the fridge purchase we discussed earlier, we give surprising credence to two sentences of feedback from someone on the other side of the world we know nothing about and we use that feedback to help narrow the otherwise overwhelming set of choices in front of us.

> We shop the global internet with technological sophistication and enthusiasm, but we shop it in essentially the same way we'd have shopped the village market 200 years ago.

Mission: Survival

Each of the rules has the potential to be scary. In each of them is a significant challenge for established retailers. Many retailers have disappeared in the last couple of decades as a result of being under-cut either by supermarkets or by 'pure-play' online-only retailers with a lower cost base and a thirst for growth. In the course of this book we'll see examples of long-established business models being challenged not by new competitors but by a new and more sophisticated understanding from consumers, driven by the freely available internet. We'll see hugely profitable start-ups popping up who will take from you only your most profitable customers and will leave you with the rest, or who will do just one of the things that you used to do for your customers but will do so with focus and precision and undercut your profitability in so doing.

One of the great tragedies of the wave of technological and business change which has flowed around the world in the last few decades is that so few incumbent businesses have successfully made those gains. Too often they have gotten stuck – hide-bound by existing processes, terrified of cannibalising long-held assets, held back by the need to constantly satisfy shareholders' short-term goals or, frankly, just not smart or nimble enough. When an existing market leader is struck down by a new start-up who began with none of the brand recognition, no customer database and no money to invest in sales or marketing it can only be a measure of failure that the new entrant could get up enough momentum in the first place.

But if the history of business teaches us one thing, it is that change is opportunity. Each of these rules contains within it massive opportunities – to find new customers, to better address existing ones and even to create whole new markets. In this book we will explore, understand and discuss the rules and what they mean for us. Then we will find those opportunities and build our plan to take advantage of them.

Those opportunities do not just need to offer themselves to shiny new start-ups. No-one has more to gain from evolving a long-established market than those who know it best. It is time for businesses to fight back – reclaiming the initiative and rebuilding their market leadership.

Navigating this book

Each of the rules of the New Normal is about change. Consumers, regulators, markets and technologies are all evolving, creating both threats and opportunities for established retail brands. Across the rest of this book we will explore how those businesses can cut through their history, conservatism and fear of change and reboot themselves to take full advantage of the opportunities which change creates. We'll look at the financial, technical and human reasons why incumbents sometimes fail to do that, and we'll explore how to capitalise on our strengths rather than being tied down by our weaknesses.

In the first part of the book we will discuss the rules of the New Normal. By understanding how the world has changed we can develop our own strategy to reclaim market leadership. We'll explore how each of these rules have come to be and their profound implications and use that insight to develop strategies that will drive commercial success in the new world. We'll also explore real-world examples to see how some leading retailers around the world have ignored the New Normal and suffered as a result, but also how others have evolved their businesses and fought back successfully against new entrants.

My objective in laying out the rules of the New Normal is a practical one. I want to provide you with tools to build a strategy which is right for your business and generates a response to the changing consumer landscape which is appropriate, proportionate and effective.

Throughout each chapter, therefore, we will take action planning breaks. Rather than wait until the end and produce a huge checklist of things to think about, it is much more practical to stop every now and again and really think through a single issue or question. Some planning exercises will take the form of discussion guides or questionnaires which you can use with your team to dig into a topic. Others will challenge whether you have the data or skills you need in your business. In all cases, they represent useful exercises you and your team can use to begin to build effective strategies for the New Normal.

Then in Part 2 of the book we'll switch from building strategy to putting it into practice. The intellectual task of working out what we *should* do is often the easiest part of creating change. Getting it to actually happen is much harder and will require us to build a powerful momentum for change.

Finding inspiration

One source of inspiration for this strategic challenge is to learn from other industries. I've had the good fortune to see at first hand not only retail and hospitality businesses but also industries like telecoms and subscription TV which have very different approaches to building relationships with customers.

As well as differences, however, there are also parallels and lessons we can learn from the approaches that work in different sectors, and our journey through this book draws on many of those.

There is plenty of cause for optimism. In retailing I've seen first hand the huge response from consumers that comes when brands embrace the lessons of the New Normal and embrace the new consumer.

But, I've also seen first hand the tragic consequences when they don't, and instead get out-competed, lose customers and ultimately fail.

The latter story of giant and long-standing retail brands disappearing from our high streets and our memories has been an all-too-frequent hallmark of the last decade. It is unacceptable – letting down shareholders, customers and most importantly many tens of thousands of long-standing employees.

> **My mission in writing *Reinventing Retail* is to offer whatever perspective I can draw from a lifetime in consumer businesses to ensure that our great retailers thrive and grow, where once they might have fallen.**

Part

1

The rules of the New Normal

Chapter

1

Rule 1: Someone is going to sell your product at cost or less

The first rule of the New Normal makes no sense at all, does it? How can it be that competitors can spring up and so massively undercut traditional retailers? After all, management textbooks talk about return on capital, and surely it can't be the case that someone can operate a business making essentially no profit year after year and yet continue to invest and grow? It defies common sense. And yet it happens over and over.

This low-price, and apparently low-profit competition can in fact spring up for several reasons:

- **A competitor might not be selling below *their* cost but just below *your* cost.** They might simply have a much lower cost base. The most obvious example here are internet 'pure-play' retailers who sprang up to compete with traditional high-street incumbents. By not having the overheads of stores and staff it was possible for them to undercut on price.

- **A competitor might have no choice but to sell at low cost.** Those same pure-play retailers often struggle to differentiate themselves on customer service (not surprisingly, if they have no staff) or on product quality. It is too easy for a web shopper to glance at prices and buy from the cheapest, creating a huge pressure on the internet retailer to be the lowest price or die.

- **A competitor is selling your core product at cost because the product is not core to them.** Supermarkets have entered many new categories over the last 20 years including mobile phones, video games and more. In each case, they have ended up pricing these new products very cheaply as a loss-leader to encourage you to buy your groceries from them.

- **A competitor is playing the 'long game'.** Some internet retailers selling at cost know that eventually the retailer with the greatest scale and the biggest customer database will end up as 'last man standing' and reap the rewards. This is a dangerous game, but if you have deep pockets, infinite patience and got into the game early, it can be a winning strategy.

The most striking example of price-based competition being forced on markets has been the emergence of price comparison websites in some industries. You'll see in the next chapter how some of those industries have brought that on themselves by trying to hide and mask their pricing, creating a market for someone to simply cut away the nonsense and allow a straightforward comparison. But whatever the root cause, once a price comparison culture has emerged in a market it becomes distinctly harder to compete on any other basis.

It is much harder to present a simple table comparing brand values or customer service quality than it is to compare prices, with the inevitable consequence that customers make their choice based on the information in front of them. If an industry involves multiple vendors selling products which are either exactly the same, or at least hard to distinguish from one another, then it is particularly vulnerable to this phenomenon.

In a sense, it doesn't matter why your competitor (or someone who never used to be a competitor but has suddenly started selling your products alongside their own) is doing so at cost price. They just are. And in many markets, they always will. Even if the fly-by-night online retailer who has undercut you on key products a few times goes bust, another will be along presently to try the same trick.

And so we have our first rule of the New Normal. Someone is going to sell your product at cost. Or even less.

The wrong answer is to ignore the problem

We do our businesses a disservice if we ignore this reality. It might be OK to be aggravated by unfair competition from retailers with no traditional position in your market. But it is not OK to pretend it isn't happening.

> **If we just redefine our market to include an ever smaller set of our 'normal' competitors, then we will blind ourselves to the trickle, and then flood, of customers who choose to do business with new entrants and in new ways.**

I once had occasion to ask a question to the management team of a retailer. This was a fundamentally good business with a long history and with a large set of well-designed and well-managed stores in several countries. It was also a business that had, at some level, acknowledged the existence of the internet and had a website selling its products in those countries too. Its product range was focused and clear and its customer base was easily defined and enthusiastic.

The question I asked was a simple one. I asked what their market share was.

The answer was fascinating. First, it was interesting that the information was not readily available in any form. This was not a management team that was used to keeping a close eye on its competitors or on trends in customer-buying patterns – a red flag for any business.

Over my career, I've observed a strong correlation between those businesses that have a clear, frequently measured and widely discussed market share report, and those that win. There are, of course, reasons why market share reports sometimes send the wrong signal. An obsessive and wrong-headed over-focus on market share can lead to price wars, for example. But that is true of any single KPI and is the reason why strong businesses use 'balanced' sets of measures. Within that balanced set, however, market share remains a galvanising metric. Are your customers choosing to do business with you, or with your rivals? Are the actions you are taking in the marketplace serving to increase your slice of the pie, or not?

Growing market share might be about encouraging customers to switch from a rival service to yours. Competitive markets like the mobile phone business often exhibit spectacularly aggressive marketing designed to generate switching – even targeting offers directly at competitor customers.

In other markets, however, the smartest way to drive up market share might be different. In the cinema business it is much easier to encourage your existing customers to visit your cinemas more often than it is to get someone who usually goes to a competitor to come to you. But by increasing the frequency of visit from your existing customers, mathematically you increase your market share because your slice of the pie grows faster than everyone else's. As such, the market share KPI still works to focus the mind even when direct switching isn't the best tactic.

Action planning

Let's start our first strategy break with this topic of market share and some key questions:

- Do you have a good measure of market share in your business?
- How frequently is it measured, and how robust is the data?
- What's an example of a decision made in the business with the specific objective of driving market share?
- Were you trying to get consumers to switch from a rival, or your existing customers to buy more often?
- Did it work? How do you know?
- For extra bonus points, how could you measure market share on a local or regional basis too?

I hope you found our first action planning break a useful exercise. If your conclusion was that you have good, granular market share information in your business, which plays a big role in your trading decisions and strategy formulation, then terrific.

If not, then you should take some time with your team to consider how such information could be gathered. Is there an industry body to which you could subscribe? Does one of the big market research businesses have a relevant tracker? Could you even generate some information yourselves through direct research?

There's also a middle ground to be concerned about. You might have some market share information which is occasional and high level – a quarterly report, for example. That might be interesting, but it isn't going to impact many real trading decisions. There's a real 'insight trap', information which is interesting but not actionable. If you are in that trap, consider how you can increase the frequency and granularity of your insight.

Beyond driving short-term trading behaviour, market share analysis is powerful for another reason. It connects you with the real behaviours demonstrated by your customers on a daily and weekly basis. It becomes obvious whether your customer base is homogeneous, essentially one great mass of people, or whether there are distinct segments in the market who behave in different ways.

Finally, a close analysis of market share along with market size is a powerful way to identify long-term trends as you come to understand whether customer behaviours and segments are changing as time goes by.

The retail team I was working with demonstrated the importance of this more strategic aspect of market share analysis when they finally laid hands on the report and showed it to me. There on the report was our business, and there were the two or three similar competing businesses on the high street. Also there on the report were the supermarkets, who had recently entered our market and had begun selling our products too.

But someone was missing. Amazon.

When I asked why the world's largest retailer, a vigorous and competitive seller of the same products as us was not even on the report, the answer was staggering. Well, I was told, they just give our products away at cost price, so there is nothing to be done about them, and so we don't include them in the report.

We had a long conversation about that. The more I dug into it, the clearer the picture became. Amazon (and by extension the other pure online retailers too) were regarded by this management team as basically cheating. They were selling products for less than our business was – and often for less than we were paying suppliers for the products in the wholesale market. Measuring and responding to their behaviour on a daily or weekly basis was simply futile.

In a sense, they didn't represent a player in the market whose share we might measure. Instead, they represented a bit of the market which had disappeared – gone forever and not worth chasing. Because we couldn't compete with them, we chose to ignore them, but by doing so instantly blinded ourselves to a key trend behaviour being exhibited by our most valuable customers.

Viewed in print, a story like that seems absurd. It is the business equivalent of the small child putting their hands in front of their eyes and assuming that you can't see them. It is also extremely dangerous – allowing the business to construct a narrower and narrower definition of its 'real' competitors, effectively choosing to swim in a smaller and smaller pond.

I've seen echoes of the same thing in many different businesses and in many different markets.

> **There is a natural human tendency to redefine the terms of the competition to one that we might win.**

The clothing retailer who sees Primark and the supermarkets selling party dresses for just a few pounds dismisses it as "not really the business we are in". The vendor of business supplies who sees their highest margin products (printer ink, anyone?) get challenged online by generic alternatives consoles themselves with the thought that no real business customer would switch to those inferior replacements.

Action planning

- Who are your 'hidden' competitors?
- When you measure market share, do you do it the same way your customers would, or have you allowed blind spots to develop?
- Ask your customers who they consider as alternatives to your brand. Who do they list? Were you surprised by any of the competitors mentioned?
- Are there brands that you are quick to discount as not really your competitors? Beware of the self-generated blind spot.

The questions about competitors and market definition in that exercise are important to discuss with your team, but they are fascinating to talk to your customers about too. There are a variety of ways to do that including the traditional and indirect methods, such as watching a focus group discussion from behind glass, but increasingly leading brands are using workshop techniques where you and your colleagues spend time on key issues like this directly with customers.

When you measure market share, you are usually measuring market size as well. In discussing with customers what they regard as alternatives to your product, you will begin to find explanations for what looks like market size increases or decreases but are actually consumers switching from products that you measure to products that you don't.

A restaurant business knows that it is competing not just with the restaurant next door but also with customers simply deciding to stay at home and cook or buy a ready meal from a supermarket. Those are not competing restaurants, but they are substitutes for the product the restaurant is selling – alternatives which offer some of the same benefits in a different way.

Working out what the substitutes for your brand are can unlock whole new commercial opportunities – just as restaurants have unlocked with home delivery businesses.

The end-result of blinding yourself to competitors or substitutes is always the same. The challenger business which disrupts your world by selling your high-margin products for next to nothing will indeed steal your customers. If you ignore them, you just end up competing in a market which is shrinking fast as customers move to the alternative.

Embracing the reality of new competition and the inevitability of many of our products being sold at or near cost is not a counsel of despair. Indeed, embracing that reality is the beginning of being able to do something about it.

There are a range of ways we can use our pricing and distribution strategies to respond to these new competitors. It might be the case that a new entrant is willing to sell a product at cost that you have been used to making a healthy margin on. But that does not mean that it is inevitable that they will succeed. In your business you have access to a range of advantages that a new entrant does not, and we will see examples throughout this book of how those advantages can be put to work to change the rules of the competitive game in your favour.

Because the beauty is that the very same forces which created at-cost competition in the first place also create the seeds of our response to that competition. Consumers' willingness to shop online, to compare prices and to buy from new and unexpected entrants to your market is one aspect of how the life of the consumer has changed in our new 'always on' 'omnichannel' world.

But this new world has changed other aspects of consumer behaviour too, and by understanding those and using them to our advantage to develop and deploy new strategies for connecting with customers, we can take control of our newly competitive markets and win market share from those new entrants rather than hiding from them.

So what can we do?

Five critical strategies to compete with low-price new entrants

Successfully competing in a market where someone is trying to sell your product at or below cost rests on a key insight. The first-order impact of the New Normal might have been to encourage a lot of new online market entrants competing on price, but we shouldn't forget the second-order impact. The New Normal has changed how consumers shop. In particular, what people are prepared to pay for has changed completely. By understanding how, we can re-engineer our product offering, pricing strategy and distribution and transform the profitability of our business.

Homer Simpson has a revelation in one of my favourite episodes of the show. Finding a $20 bill when looking for a peanut, his inner voice deals with his disappointment by reminding him that "money can be exchanged for goods and services". Trust that show, of all others, to boil the whole of business down into eight words. Ultimately, in a free market people will indeed exchange money for goods and services, but with one key reality check. They will only do so when they value those goods and services more highly than they value the money they are handing over.

So far, that's market economics 101.

The key insight for retailers is that what people value in the New Normal is different than it was 20 years ago.

It is important to be clear that it is not just that our interest in buying some products has gone up, while for other products it has gone down. Even for an individual purchase, our willingness to pay for different component parts of the product or service has changed too.

Let's work an example. When you buy a chocolate bar you are actually exchanging money for a complex set of goods and services:

- The chocolate itself
- The design work, branding and marketing which has gone into creating a 'product' out of simple chocolate
- The packaging
- The cost of getting the bar from a factory somewhere into your hands
- The cost of the retail space where the bar was displayed, hoping you would notice it just when you were feeling in need of a snack
- The profit that various businesses are hoping to make from the deal, including the manufacturer, the retailer and the transport company

And the same is true for any other product or service. What seems to be a simple purchase is really a complex bundle of transactions. You are not just buying a product, you are buying the experience of having that product right now, at this time and in this place.

As markets have evolved in the New Normal, many aspects of these bundles of transactions have changed. If you don't value the design, packaging and branding in a product then there are probably low-cost versions available with generic brands and plain packaging.

If you don't value the immediacy of buying the product right now you can probably get it delivered from a warehouse tomorrow for less. If you don't value the 'discovery' and 'experience' elements of retail distribution then you can type the product's name into a search engine directly instead.

And so it is that even with products that consumers continue to buy in large volumes, it might be that the industries which create, distribute and retail those products are forced to change beyond recognition.

That change will take different forms in different industries. In some industries, for example, design, branding and a feeling of premium and exclusivity are still really important to consumers, meaning that brands which invest heavily in these areas can attract a big premium and have a strong defensible market position (think perfume).

In other sectors, however, that premium has been challenged by brands simply by-passing all of that investment and producing lower priced alternatives. Even industries which thought they were immune to that kind of competition, such as clothing and shoe businesses, have seen huge challenges from low-price alternatives, as the growth of fast fashion over the last decade illustrates.

The right product, pricing and distribution strategies for your business therefore depend on a close analysis of all the individual elements of the transaction you are asking your customer to make when they buy from you. We need, in particular, to be clear and honest with ourselves about which of those elements have changed as the world has entered the New Normal, and what that tells us about the strategy which will maximise our competitive strength and profitability.

> **A rapid and insight-led response to changes in the things customers are prepared to pay for can generate profits in the unlikeliest places.**

Here, then, are five ways in which the New Normal has changed what consumers are willing to pay for. Each of them offers a strategic opportunity to out-compete the online pure-plays and earn margin where we have not earned it before. They are the core of our response to the first rule of the New Normal.

Strategy 1: Immediacy and scarcity matter more in the New Normal

One of the things that customers will sometimes pay for is the right to have a product right now, when they want it, without waiting. And that insight leads to our first strategy.

Later when we look at distribution strategy we will analyse the different pricing strategies followed by retailers in travel hubs like airports (where we generally don't have much choice) versus on the high street (where we do). No surprise that they charge significantly more when we have fewer alternative choices.

This kind of location-based pricing demonstrates a big opportunity for many industries in the New Normal to price around availability, scarcity, exclusivity and immediate gratification.

If you have the only stock available of an in-demand product, or you are selling tickets to see the new must-see show or film, or you simply have food and drink available where there are few other outlets, then you have an opportunity to earn a return from that.

The opportunities presented by understanding the occasions when your business has some immediacy and scarcity to offer your customers, and pricing accordingly, can be transforming. One consumer business I worked with began to price products which were in short supply and in demand higher, while at the same time discounting where demand was softer. The impact was immediate (our profit grew by nearly 40%) with almost all the growth attributable to the pricing strategy. There was some consumer backlash, of course, from customers who were used to paying fixed and predictable prices, but as we'll discuss a little later on, this was manageable and temporary.

If your margins are low, and particularly if you are under pressure to sell your products at or near cost when competition from internet vendors is high, then finding those remaining, occasional opportunities to earn a premium is of critical importance.

Perhaps the clearest example of a business fighting back by pricing based on scarcity and immediacy is the UK newsagent WH Smith. By nimbly increasing prices for those products where it has become the last retailer on the high street, and by adopting different pricing strategies in different types of location (airports, motorway services, railway stations), it has grown its profit year over year. And that is despite operating in some very challenging categories like confectionary and books where it faces significant competition from online retailers, supermarkets and other specialists. It hasn't always been a popular strategy, but it has been a very effective one. Theirs is a case study we'll return to in a later chapter.

It is well worth reviewing your sales with your leadership team through this lens. Look at sales by different customer types, different product types, different days, different times of day, different locations and through different channels. Ask yourselves on each occasion whether you have an opportunity to earn a return through offering customers immediacy, selling them something in short supply or finding a buying occasion where, frankly, they don't have many alternatives.

You will then need to think carefully about the most honest, transparent and practical way to make that happen without causing a big campaigning customer backlash. As we will discuss at length later, customers in the New Normal are very able to amplify complaints online. Notwithstanding that, there is nothing to be ashamed of about earning a profit where you can, and particularly where you have worked hard to put yourself in a position of having something to sell that others don't.

Sometimes whole industries which have grown up before the New Normal have developed a blind spot around pricing. Few chain restaurants vary their prices enough from town to town based on the level of competition and the ability of consumers to pay. In the UK, some will have London and non-London pricing but that doesn't begin to maximise the potential returns. Similarly, few chain restaurants will vary their pricing from day to day across the week (indeed, with printed menus most can't) or between busier and quieter parts of the year. A few might have higher prices around Christmas or big national events like Thanksgiving in the US, but again those are baby steps compared to the potential returns from a more granular review of pricing.

The same is true in many other industries. A sense of how it's always been done prevents them from looking really forensically at the margin-enhancing opportunities which might be there for some products, in some places, at some times.

And you will also need to ensure you do the ground work to build a consensus for change inside your own business. If the organisation at large is nervous about adopting a more variable pricing policy of the kind we've talked about here, it will tend to passively resist it. The business I worked with which implemented variable pricing saw exactly that (although it is fair to say the resistance crumbled a bit when the profit grew so much).

It will be important to ensure that the teams who have to make the pricing changes understand the benefits in doing so (and in particular, that if you make a profit by pricing a particular sale as high as you can, you are earning the resources to price another sale in a more competitive market more keenly).

> **It is vital that the front-line teams who deal with customers every day understand what you are doing and why, so that they can represent your brand honestly and with integrity to your customers.**

In the experiment with variable pricing that I referred to before, we spent as much time making sure that the new pricing policy made sense to colleagues and customers as we did doing the maths to get the prices themselves. In Part 2 we will explore some powerful practical checklists for building the kind of internal consensus and understanding that a change like this needs in order to really stick.

Indeed, as we'll see in Chapter 2, not every way we could make money in the short term by playing with our prices will necessarily maximise the longer-term value of our business. Here, we will build our list of ways that we *could* vary our prices, but later we'll refine that down to the list of ways we *should* vary them.

Figure 1.1 Factors affecting pricing

Action planning

Pricing strategy in the New Normal is about detail.

- You obviously have different prices for different products, but do you vary prices on any of these dimensions:
  - product availability
  - the intensity of the competition for a particular product
  - region or town/city

- day of the week or time of day
- the age or demographic of the customer
- the volume of product being purchased
- the value of the customer, expressed by the amount of other things they buy from you.
- If you don't vary prices on some of these dimensions, what would happen if you did?
- If you do vary prices on these dimensions, how do you know you are getting the balance right? If you chose to reduce your discount for teens, for example, how would you measure the impact?

Strategy 2: A different or better product changes the competitive playing field

The pricing strategy review we've just been through is about finding those specific occasions when, either by having a product no one else makes or by having something for sale at exactly the moment your customer needs it, you have a temporary competitive advantage.

There is, of course, one fundamental, powerful and sustainable source of competitive advantage, and that is to simply have a better product than your competitors.

Whether of higher quality, with additional extras, of better design or differentiated in any number of other ways, there are certainly markets where businesses have been able to sustain themselves against a mass of low-cost online competitors and thrive.

Consider the chocolate retailer Hotel Chocolat. Not only does it have a high-quality product to begin with, but it also continues to innovate and launch new lines all the time. As a result, it has resisted the competition from supermarkets which has undone some of its confectionary competitors.

Sometimes, when we think of product differentiation we come up with examples in high-end industries such as luxury goods, designer labels and exclusive products. That doesn't necessarily have to be the case, however. Many brands have managed to build strong market positions in their sectors while resolutely addressing the mass market.

It could seem obvious that making sure your product is differentiated from your competition, and seen by customers as better, is a good thing. Yet, there are a striking range of examples where incumbent businesses have faced competition from lower-cost new entrants but have failed to use differentiation as a tool to strike back.

Sometimes differentiation can be difficult, particularly where complex production processes are involved, but that doesn't always need to be the case. Simply reformulating, repackaging or innovating through new colours or other variants can create enough points of difference to keep customers interested. Just ask big branded consumer goods businesses, which are locked into an endless innovation race with me-too competitors who will bring out suspiciously similarly packaged shampoos or soap powders and try to compete on price. Over the years, the big incumbents have become very good indeed at keeping customers through a continual flow of innovation.

It is well worth considering how you can use innovation and product differentiation to help win the battle with your retail competitors. Can you leverage your relationship with suppliers to source innovative variants of best-selling lines? Can you offer different or hard-to-find stock variants that the online warehouses don't?

Alternatively, can you bundle products together in interesting and innovative ways – something that can simultaneously create a differentiated offering and increase customer spend? If you are a restaurant business, how often do you change your menu? Market-leading casual dining chains like Wagamama have generated considerable customer loyalty and revenue growth in recent years from menu innovation done really carefully, with new dishes first tested as specials and then made standard or culled based on customer feedback.

Often the truth is that we aren't innovating or improving our products and services as much as our customers would like, because we are limited by our internal processes, resource constraints or even by our company culture. Working backwards from a desire to innovate more can result in some powerful business change programmes. Later we'll look at how we can create a climate in a business which encourages and rewards small, easy experimentation that can drive innovation.

Action planning

The same technological changes which created the New Normal also create the potential to dramatically speed up our product development and innovation processes – and doing so is a powerful way to escape from price competition.

- Create with your team a list of the ways (big and small) in which you might create innovation in your business.

- Examples include varying colours and styles of product, creating limited editions, varying designs or specifications.

- Plot those on the chart below to identify quick wins and long-term strategy opportunities.

- Be careful not to accept any organisational blind spots in this exercise. Try to use verifiable data to justify where you are placing each option on the chart.

- Having created and debated the chart, some options for 'big bang for the buck' product or service differentiation should emerge. They will contain the beginnings of a fight back against vanilla low-cost competitors.

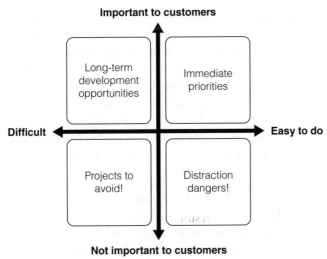

Figure 1.2 Mapping potential innovation ideas

Strategy 3: In an online, connected world the wisdom of the crowd is powerful and your existing customers are a huge asset

In his magnificent book *Influence,* American social scientist Robert Cialdini observes a series of fascinating things about human behaviour. We are essentially tribal. We are comfortable when the things we are doing are similar to the things that the people around us are doing.

You can see this behaviour all around you. In his book, Cialdini cites an experiment originally carried out in the 1960s in New York where some volunteers were asked to stand on the street staring up at the sixth-floor window of a nearby building. The behaviour of the 'real' people walking past on the busy street was then tracked. If you put a single volunteer looking up at the window, most people walking past just ignore them.

Adding a second student, so that there are now two people staring at the roof has much the same effect. But add a third, fourth or fifth and something interesting happens. A passer-by stops, curious about what they are looking at, and looks up him or herself. So now there are more people there, and soon a crowd has formed. The more people there are around us doing something, the more we want to do the same thing ourselves. After all, everyone else can't be wrong, can they?

In running a retail business, a similar effect is easy to observe. I remember once opening a newly refurbished and redesigned store for a big global brand. As it happened, this was also the first day at work for the new chairman of this massive company, and he decided that what he wanted to do on his first day was see this store re-opened. Of course, the chairman of a big public company doesn't just arrive on his own, especially on his first day, so an entourage of Important People arrived too. We cut the ribbon and opened the store, and I went outside to see what it looked like from the street.

Horrified, I realised that the store was packed to the gills with Important People in grey suits all chatting to each other. This was a disaster – seeing the store full, surely no real customers would bother to walk in – there was a danger that our new chairman would see a new store take no business.

I could not have been more wrong. Far from putting people off, the bustle in the store attracted them in, and soon we were doing a roaring trade.

The lesson I learned that day I've seen again dozens of times since.

> **The busier a store is, the more people want to come inside.**

It is as if the ice is broken. The crowd indicates that there must be good things on sale, and so everyone wants to join in. I've even seen the same effect on a market stall, which had either no customers or far too many as a result. This insight explains why a good restaurant will always seat customers in the window first to create the sense that you are missing out by not being in there yourself.

It is undeniable that, in general, we want to do what others do, buy what others buy, eat what others eat and so on. But this psychology is often overlooked as a competitive weapon. Consider your business. How can you create scale effects where the sheer number of customers you have attracts others, and helps you to fend off attacks from new entrants in your market who, by definition, don't have that scale when they start.

It might be by having a thriving social media presence where customers can see for themselves how many other people use and value your service. It might be by deliberate marketing based on your scale (millions of people enjoy brand x). One way or another, if you have a big customer base it is worth really thinking through how you can use it to both attract and retain business.

One of the most powerful ways of doing that which the New Normal offers us is to use the wisdom of the crowd to get customers to help each other. A business like TripAdvisor, with a huge number of restaurant and hotel reviews, has a natural defence against a new entrant springing up. If I want to read reviews, I go where the reviews are. If I'm then going to leave a review of my own, I will probably leave it in the same place. This is scale-economics in action.

I've seen businesses with large customer service operations (like mobile phone businesses) do this in a very clever way. By creating an online customer service forum where smart super-user customers can show off by solving complex problems for other customers, they achieve three things. First, there is the cost saving from reduced calls into the call centre. Second, there is the direct customer satisfaction created for the customer having their problem solved. But third, there is the opportunity for millions of other customers, current and potential, to see that advice being delivered and use it for themselves. Once again, the internet allows a business not just to deliver great service (or in this case have its customers do that for it) but also to be seen to deliver that service by lots of other people.

Even if a self-help forum like that is available to non-customers too, it still helps to reinforce that this particular brand is 'where it's all happening' and create the sense that if everyone else is there, I want to be there too.

What is the equivalent in your industry? If you have scale, how can you turn it into a competitive advantage by making sure that your customers don't want to miss out on what everyone else is enjoying?

Strategy 4: In the New Normal, consumers value experiences as well as products

To see the long-term impact of the New Normal there is no better thing to do than to look to consumers who have grown up with it. Whether you badge them Gen Y, Gen Z, millennials or anything else, there is a young generation now grown into adults who have lived in the always-on, perfect-information chaos of the New Normal almost their whole lives. They are hardly a homogeneous mass, and it is a mistake to treat all young people as somehow identical, but by looking at how they shop and consume, and the things they choose to pay for (and not) we can learn a lot about the future.

To create our fourth strategy for coping with at-cost pricing, there is one particularly interesting and consistent aspect of millennial behaviour, and that is the search for the experience. When all products are available cheaply and conveniently, the consumption of products no longer becomes the thing that separates one person from another. You aren't interesting because you own something, when anyone else who wanted it could also own it.

The scarcity that millennials seek is often the experience rather than the possession.

Owning the new album is irrelevant. Having been to the concert or the festival where the band played, however, is not. Seeing the movie is easy. Going to the secret screening where everyone dressed up and there was a Q&A with the director, however, is a big deal.

The cinema industry offers some great examples. There has been huge growth in 'event' cinema experiences where people dress up to view classic films, and there are a range of other special experiences such as preview screenings, screenings with introductions by film-makers, even 'blind' screenings where a new film is shown but the audience doesn't know in advance what it is going to see. All of these add value to what might otherwise be a humdrum, repeatable, undifferentiated experience.

And where millennials go, the rest of us follow. Whether it is creating our own holidays by booking the component parts ourselves rather than going on the same package trip as everyone else, or the growth in pop-up fashion and food outlets, consumers are placing more and more value on experiences which are hard to replicate, personal to them and give them something to tweet about.

It is well worth considering how this works in your industry. What transient, personal, tweet-worthy experiences can you create? And if the answer is that the creation of these experiences is irrelevant to your business, just remember that the simple act of putting names on to Cola bottles created huge noise for one big brand, and sold a lot of fizzy drink.

Strategy 5: The more personalised our products and services, the less exposed we are to price competition

If we take this trend towards wanting experiences that help us stand out from the crowd to its logical extent, then there is nothing so unique as a product or experience which has been created especially for us.

Whether it is clothing which is made to fit you, not made to fit some mythical standard size, or paint for your room mixed in a colour you created, there is undeniable value in the exclusive, unique and personal. For an established brand fending off competition from bulk-manufacturing, low-cost, me-too new entrants, there can be no better example of the benefits of scale, industry knowledge and expertise than creating bespoke products and experiences for customers.

Historically, this would have been an option open to only very few businesses that catered for the top end of luxury markets. Now, however, some of the technological innovations we've seen emerge in the New Normal come to the rescue.

> **In a world of 3D printing, robot manufacturing lines, dynamically rendered online content and even Artificial Intelligence, what is to stop us from creating a personal product for each one of our customers?**

I learned the power of computing to personalise the hard way. As a young marketing director, I was responsible for sending direct mail (in the form of letters, postcards and magazines) to millions of customers encouraging them to buy additional products from my company. I met another such marketing director from a different brand, and we started to compare statistics. It turned out that we had similarly sized customer bases to mail (somewhere between 10 and 20 million customers each – these were big brands).

I proudly boasted that our mailshots to our huge customer base were divided into six segments. In other words, we understood our customers sufficiently well to recognise that not everyone is the same and we divided the base into segments who were likely to be similar to each other, manually produced six different versions of each communication and sent different ones to the different segments. Letters to older and less affluent customers would be worded differently to those sent to young families, for example.

Having told my story, I asked my counterpart how many different letters he would send to his 20 million customers. The answer was

20 million different letters. His business understood its customers (and their historic purchases) so incredibly well that it was able to customise a letter and the attached offers and vouchers precisely for that customer to maximise the value it was delivering and the chance of a response.

Well, that told me. These days, that feat is not nearly as impressive as it was 15 years ago. Modern computer systems, aligned to digital printing technology, can deliver customised versions of marketing material (or emails, more often) at relatively low cost.

But what is now normal in the creation of advertising is not so common in the creation of the products themselves. The advertising coming through my door or arriving in my email inbox is very highly targeted, but the newspapers and magazines I get delivered are not. Yet there is no logical barrier to a newspaper company allowing me to tailor the kind of articles I want in my newspaper and printing an edition customised just for me. Is there?

The opportunity that new technology offers us to customise and personalise our products and services for our customers is present in many markets now but exploited in few. Consider clothing. My generation was brought up with the idea of standard sizes and the sense that if you wanted a dress or a suit made specifically for your personal measurements, that was possible only at the highest end of the market and only in return for thousands of pounds. But is that still true? Is there not an opportunity for clothing brands to gather the measurements of customers and use robotic production lines to create individual garments for them?

Consider also home furnishing. Why do I have to worry about whether that particular sofa will fit in my living room, or whether the colour will match my other furniture, when it would be perfectly possible for one to be made in exactly the size and colour I need.

In all of the product categories we've discussed here, and more, innovative start-up businesses are exploring exactly this kind of personalisation. A small but interesting example is the online and retail business Duoboots who make, as the name implies, fashionable ladies boots. Unlike larger bootmakers, Duoboots not only sell boots in different shoe sizes but also in different widths, different calf sizes and different materials, meaning the product each customer buys is much more personally tailored for her. It's a recipe for higher customer satisfaction and more return business.

But what a tragedy it would be if this kind of personalisation became another problem for incumbent big businesses to worry about, when in fact it should be exactly the weapon they need to continue to attract customers and charge premium prices against low-cost new entrants.

There is a real danger for retailers that they end up stuck in the middle of a polarisation of new technology. On the one hand, low-cost online players undercutting them on price for their standard products, and at the other end of the spectrum the creation of experiences, personalised and unique left to other new entrants with a focus on the latest technology. As we've seen so far, there is an opportunity for the existing incumbent to bravely embrace either or both ends of this spectrum, not just to leave the playing field open to others.

Another strategy to avoid – asking the wrong question

We've just been through a rich set of ways that a retailer can avoid being dragged into pricing at cost. So what's stopping us? Why do long-established retailers persistently fail to compete successfully with new digital entrants in their markets?

There are many things that stop big businesses re-inventing themselves in the New Normal, but the biggest barriers are human ones. When we've worked in an industry for a long time, it can be difficult to see how dramatically it has changed, and difficult to lift our eyes and see the wider picture.

As an example, you can hear this very human phenomenon when you listen to the objections that some retail businesses raise to investing in e-commerce in response to new entrants selling products for much lower prices. Here is a question I've heard a dozen times: "Doesn't e-commerce just cannibalise my business, moving high-margin sales into a low-margin channel?"

It is worth thinking hard about this because it is looking at the world the wrong way round. The profitability of an individual sales channel is increasingly irrelevant for most businesses, particularly since most customers will use several channels in a purchase process. They might check stock levels and prices on the web before visiting a store to touch and feel the product and then buy from the web anyway so that they don't need to carry shopping bags home.

In such a world, the margin that appears to be generated by an individual sales channel can be deeply misleading.

The correct question to ask is about the profitability of individual customers, not individual sales channels.

After all, you operate shops to do business with customers, not for their own sake. Some of our most forward-thinking retailers are already contemplating the possibility of stores existing mainly as conduits for web sales.

If you don't embrace the web as a sales channel, and your competitors do, then you miss out on a lot more than "some revenue that was going to be low margin anyway". You also begin to lose your most valuable customers as they are attracted to rivals who will do business with them through the channels they want to use.

The customer who wants to shop both online and in store will shift to a retailer who gives that choice. As a consequence, 'stores only' businesses lose high-margin customers. The paradox is that by trying to protect your traditional retail margin, you end up watching your stores become less and less profitable.

This channel-focused behaviour is deeply ingrained for many retailers. Even those who believe that they understand the importance of measuring value by customer are probably still sitting down every week to review a margin report which starts by splitting out each channel. Those reports do that not because it is right but because it is easy to measure.

Bringing it together

So, there we have it. In the New Normal, what people are prepared to pay for has changed. The smart response to the rise of low-price competitors is to look at your pricing and product development strategies through a different lens. To figure out how you can earn margin in ways, and in places, that your competitors cannot.

Interestingly, only a small part of the correct strategic response to competitors selling at cost is about your pricing. By broadening our analysis to better understand why people are prepared to pay different amounts for different things at different times, we've unlocked ways in which our distribution, product development, customer service and innovation strategies can help us earn a margin too.

In laying out these five strategies, we've created the outline of a fundamental review of your pricing and margin management. The key tasks we've created are:

- Reviewing the opportunities for variable pricing in your business. Can you vary pricing by outlet, product scarcity, the day of the week or time of day or on any other dimension which might allow you to find margin?

- Finding opportunities for product innovation. How can we differentiate our product versus our competitors or even simply increase the range of choices and the pace of change so that we always have something new to talk about? What are the process and technological barriers to innovating more quickly in our business and how do we overcome them?

- Creating value from scale. If we are a big player in our market, how can we make a virtue of that? How can we enlist the customers we already have to make ourselves a better or easier business for new customers to do business with?

- Unlocking the power of experiences. How can we build experience into our customer offering to give customers a reason to do business with us?

- Personalisation. Can we deliver a more individual and personal experience to our customers, not just in the marketing materials we send them but also in our products themselves? What are the 'standard size, standard colour' limitations in our industry and how can we use our scale and technology to shatter them?

Each of these topics is worth time in its own right. Scarcity, product differentiation, social proof, the experience of being your customer and the uniqueness and personalisation of your product are all things that you ask customers to implicitly pay for when they buy from you.

By understanding how the New Normal and the rise of new competitors in your industry has impacted the willingness of your customers to pay for these hidden aspects of your product, you can identify powerful ways to compete with those competitors.

A project plan checklist

- Do you understand all the details of how your pricing works now? Does it vary by sales channel, customer demand level, stock quantity, the day of the week or time of year?

- Have you reviewed what would happen if you did vary prices on some of these dimensions? Are there operational issues to be overcome? What might customer reactions be? Critically, what would the margin impact be?

- Do you have the analytical skills in your business to carry out this kind of analysis reliably? If not, where can you find it?

- Do you have a customer-led view of how your product compares with competitors? Are you relying on differentiators that no longer matter to customers?

- How could you increase the pace and effectiveness of innovation in your product set? Could you source from new places? If you manufacture, is there a way to tool your production more quickly? How might you use a faster pace of innovation to create distance from your competitors?

- Do you charge a premium over generic and unbranded competitors? If so, do you deserve it? If not, how might you add to the customer experience until you do?

- If you have a lot of customers and face competition from new entrants who don't, do you have a strategy for how you can make your scale work to your advantage?

▶

- How can you create meaningful and transient experiences for your customers that will give them more than just the basic experience of buying your product? How can you make your retail space one which is actually rewarding to visit? Are there services you can offer alongside your core product set?
- What would your product or service look like if it was genuinely personalised to an individual customer? What would your business look like if it was capable of delivering that?

Working this through might result in you reworking your pricing strategy to get the most from every sale. It might encourage you to invest in technology to increase the pace of your product innovation or to give you the ability to personalise products for individual customers. It might make you think about creating experiences, building fan clubs, creating online customer forums where consumers can advise and help each other. You might renew your packaging, your branding or your customer promises.

And in each of these actions lies the opportunity to take the commercial agenda back from those online warehouses.

Far from the New Normal being a recipe for everything being sold at cost, it has created a myriad of ways in which you can continue to give customers what they want and earn a margin from doing so. They are just new ways, requiring new approaches.

And all of that opportunity came just from the first rule of the New Normal. Next we'll explore the second rule. If it isn't bad enough that you now face competition from new entrants willing to sell your core products at cost or less, you also do so in a world where customers know everything, and all your proprietary secrets are out.

Chapter

Rule 2: Everyone knows everything – nothing is a secret

It is a tough business, making money. Ultimately, there has to be some reason why people will buy your product from you for more than it costs you to make, distribute or retail it. Economists call that a 'competitive advantage' and having one is a critical ingredient to being able to run a successful and sustainable retail business.

Sometimes competitive advantage is about costs. You might have a scale advantage over competitors, simply making or buying so much of a product or running a process on such a high volume that your costs are lower and you can charge a keener price than anyone else. You might have based your business in a lower cost market or have access to some proprietary technology that allows you the same benefit. You might even simply have a managerial edge over your competitors, able to organise your business to do the same things but more effectively and efficiently than anyone else can.

This cost-related type of competitive advantage (often called 'comparative advantage') is very often a key engine of competition in a market. In fact, it is so important to world trade that economists often use the language of comparative advantage to describe patterns of international trade between countries themselves. We've all seen over the last few decades how the rise in high-quality but low-cost manufacturing in developing markets has forced whole industries to relocate, costing jobs in more developed markets where living costs are higher.

The response of those developed countries, however, illustrates a different type of competitive advantage. Industrialised, developed countries can no longer sustain industries where cost is the most important determinant of success. Those industries, and the jobs they created, have long migrated to developing markets where people will work for a few dollars a day and where, therefore, products can be made for a fraction of the cost and sold on the world market. The cost differences can be huge. I've seen more than one business where it proved to be cheaper to ship finished products to China to have some basic final task completed (putting the product into its packaging, for example) and ship them back again, than it was to pay to have that task completed locally.

The smart response for a nation which sees its traditional industries migrating to the developed world is not to wish that they would come back. That trend is irreversible. Instead, it is to focus efforts, investment and resources into activities and industries where the richer nation still has an advantage. That advantage won't be about cost though.

So how can a first-world, developed nation compete on the world market against other nations with much lower industrial cost bases? One answer is innovation. By inventing new products, creating patents and other types of intellectual property, the developed nation can sell products and services where it can't be undercut by the lower-cost competitors. Another and often related answer is design and quality. By making products that are simply different to their low-cost alternatives and which customers value, a developed economy can sustain an industrial base that isn't so vulnerable to price-based competition.

The car industry gives us a terrific example of this global game of high-stakes economic chess in action. Once upon a time, the developed economies of the west could manufacture cars safe in the knowledge that potentially much lower-cost competitor countries did not have the facilities, the infrastructure or the educated workforce which was necessary to even enter that market. As time went by though, that all changed and today we see cars being made in a wide variety of developing markets in south-east Asia and South America.

The established players in Europe, the US and Japan can't hope to compete with these new entrants on a low-cost basis, but they also haven't disappeared. Instead, they have focused on quality, design and continuous innovation and brand-building to continue to compete for that part of the customer base which values those things. That has not been a smooth process, and the western automotive industry has had a very challenging last few decades, but the fact that the car manufacturers are still there and still standing tells us something important about competitive advantage. It isn't all about costs and about selling at the lowest possible price.

If that is true at a global level as countries and industries battle it out, it is also true for our businesses.

> **If your customers continue to buy from you and you are not the lowest-cost operator in your industry, then it must be for some other reason.**

It might be a design, invention or patent that no one else has. It might be about the quality and training of your people. It might be that you have invested in building a brand that your customers recognise and trust. It might be because of the quality of your after-sales care or because the experience of doing business with you is a positive and rewarding one.

Action planning

What are the sources of your business's competitive advantage? Consider the following:

1. You are the only place customers can buy the products you sell without taking an inconvenient journey to a competitor.
2. You are cheaper than your competitors because you have a cost advantage.
3. Your brand is stronger and better known than your competitors.
4. The product niche you occupy is not a major focus for any of your competitors and so you attract customers through your specialisation and expertise.

▶

5. You have a better, broader or more authoritative product range than your competitors.

6. Your shops or website are easier to navigate, do a better job of showing off products to their best advantage or are otherwise more attractive than your competitors.

7. Your customers come to you through inertia – they have alternatives but haven't really taken advantage of them yet.

8. You are able to exploit breadth of range versus more specialist retailers, offering bundles and cross-sale promotions that attract customers.

9. Your customers are committed to your brand commercially – they might be holders of loyalty cards with lots of points, or subscribers or members of your 'club'.

You'll notice in this exercise that there is a mixture between sources of competitive advantage that are down to your own actions, and those which are arguably fortuitous and the result of competitor inaction or customer inertia. As you review this with your team, be honest with yourselves about what you think drives your business today.

Then explore these two follow-up questions:

- How did you know the answer to the question? Was it gut-feel, experience-based or do you have research and customer feedback that provides evidence? If it was the former, it is well worth considering how to gather some empirical data about how customers choose to shop with you or your competitors. You might be surprised by the results.

- Then, once you are happy you have a view of today's competitive advantage, consider how you are going to grow and protect it. What competitive changes might cause customers to reconsider? If your competitive advantage feels transient and unstable, what new reasons can you create for customers to choose to do business with you?

Some of the drivers of competitive advantage will come up again as we go through this book and in particular we will look at the power of location. It is well worthwhile though, taking a moment just to baseline what your business thinks are the reasons customers shop with you, and also to think about whether that view is evidence-based or in danger of being a corporate blind spot.

So far so good. But be careful. Of all the reasons why your customers continue to do business with you rather than chasing the lowest price in town, some are more stable and more defend-able than others.

> **Do you succeed with your customers because of the outstanding service you offer or because you just happen to be the only business they can conveniently buy from?**

This is never truer than in retailing. Many large retail businesses convinced themselves that the number of customers walking through their doors was proof that they were doing a great job, only to come badly unstuck when the internet and the arrival of giant supermarkets into new product categories took away their historical local monopoly.

There is a big difference between a loyal customer base and one which is just resigned and compliant. Later we'll explore how the key historical driver of profit for many retailers – location – has changed beyond all recognition.

Knowledge is power

The arrival of the internet has dramatically altered another historical driver of profitability for businesses. Once upon a time, it was possible to make money simply because you had access to knowledge that your customers did not. Earlier we saw a great example of this.

It used to be very difficult for consumers to compare with each other the prices they were being charged for services like insurance and energy. Unlike retail products in a shop where the price ticket is on display to everyone and we all basically pay the same price for the same goods, these financial and energy products are harder to compare. I probably don't use electricity in my house in exactly the same way and to the same extent that you do, and in any case who wants to pore through the details of their neighbour's electricity bills in the first place? The internet changed all of that, and it did so in two key ways.

First, the difficulty of sharing information between customers is massively reduced now. Economists talk about 'transaction costs' to mean not just a physical monetary cost of doing something, but also the hassle, the time and the difficulty of doing something. One of the most far-reaching impacts of our new always-on internet-connected world is that it has massively reduced the transaction costs of sharing information across large groups of people.

One of my favourite examples of Twitter in action was the emergence of the #uksnow hashtag where people spontaneously share their postcode and some information about how intensely it is snowing. A simple program trawling that hashtag can create a real-time map of snow moving across the country, which for a nation as weather-obsessed as the UK is a dangerous drug indeed.

If it's that easy for thousands of people to tell each other whether it is snowing or not, it is equivalently easy for them to share information about whether they think their car insurance is a rip-off. Indeed, the clearest example of this kind of information-sharing made easy is the emergence of price comparison sites. Just fill in a few bits of information about your electricity and gas usage and see all the offers from potential providers laid out in front of you.

In dozens of markets, whether through this kind of formal comparison or just through consumers being able to communicate more easily and more spontaneously on social media, industry 'norms' have been challenged. We don't just compare electricity bills. Broadband speeds, holiday prices, airline ticket charges, restaurant reviews and a host of other databases of information are at our fingertips. If you are old enough to remember choosing a hotel or a restaurant without having thousands of other consumers' opinions at your fingertips then you'll also remember how much easier it was for these businesses to get away with lower standards of service. We'll explore that in depth in a case study later.

If the internet reduced the 'transaction cost' of sharing information with each other about businesses, it also changed the consumer landscape in another powerful way. It equipped us to do something with the information we now possess. It made us activists.

A long time ago, in the pre-internet world, I worked with a business which was based on subscriptions – regular monthly payments. The economics of the business worked in very much the same way as the utility companies we've talked about, which inevitably meant that we had a huge incentive to give our very best deals to those customers who were most at risk of leaving, and our worst deals to those who just quietly went on paying their subscription each month. Indeed, our very best deals were often sent out in paper mailshots (remember those) to customers who had recently quit their subscriptions in the hope that they might come back.

The transaction cost for a consumer of sharing that information widely was quite high. We'd get examples of our generous 'come back' offer letter being taken into work and posted on the factory bulletin board for everyone else to take advantage of, but that was manageable, local and limited.

How the world has now changed. Not only do we now see those behaviours clearly highlighted on social media and on campaigning websites, but we can do something about it with the click of a button. It is so easy to retweet a hashtag or like a campaigning Facebook page that the economics of things like subscription businesses have entirely changed. New business models have sprung up guaranteeing that existing long-standing customers will always get the best deals and they have done so not because of innate generosity from business leaders but as a result of consumer action.

And it is not just subscription businesses which have been challenged by a new world of perfect information. Consider the garage which fits a part to your car or the plumber who fits a part to your boiler. The wholesale cost of that part was once a mystery but is now very easy to find out online. Indeed, if you are brave or foolish enough, there will also be YouTube videos galore with step-by-step instructions on fitting the part yourself, part of a trend of disintermediation which we will talk about later.

So here is our second rule of the New Normal. Everyone knows everything, and it is impossible to build a business based on proprietorial knowledge or treating one group of customers differently to others.

No bad thing, I say. None of the historical business practices which we have discussed should make anyone nostalgic. The reality is that giving your best deal to your least loyal customers was always a terrible business practice and never created the lasting relationship between business and customer that great brands are built on.

> **There is a big difference between "That used to be a great business model" and "We used to get away with it".**

The greater visibility of your pricing models, the greater clarity about what you paid for the part you are fitting and the much faster and more vigorous response from groups of customers who feel they have been unfairly treated might all have been amplified by the internet, but they were always there.

But while we can welcome this new openness and clarity (particularly as consumers ourselves), we also have to acknowledge that it has changed the rules for many businesses in many industries, and that some of our historical sources of profit might be gone forever.

Again, that is no reason to be disheartened. The same sharing of information and social network tribalism that penalises perceived unfair behaviour by businesses can also laud and support fair, open and honest business dealing. If there is an aspect of your market which consumers increasingly and vocally dislike, there is money to be made by championing change. Businesses which are the first to own a customer pain-point and visibly do something about it can gain hugely from the consumer response that follows.

Action planning

What is the customer pain-point in your industry? What are the common gripes that customers complain about?

Here's a handy way to think about that. If there are things about your industry that often come up in casual conversation when you meet new people, they are likely to be pain-points. It might be: "Oh, you work in industry X! I've never understood why the cancellation charges are so high", or "I've never understood why you don't stock more different colours or sizes", or "I can never find what I'm looking for in your store."

The same is true when you look at online discussions about your brand or your industry. If the same gripes come up over and over again, then those are what we are categorising here as 'pain-points'.

An even bigger red flag is if you find yourself, when challenged with those pain-points, trying to explain them away as inevitable features of the industry: "Ah, what you don't understand is that the regulator makes us do that" or "It's because of the pressures to keep prices down" or "It's to prevent fraud."

In fact, almost any time you end up saying to a customer something that begins with "I hear you, but the reason is . . . " you are defending a pain-point, rather than listening to it.

Once you have identified your customer pain-points, a fascinating thought experiment is to ask yourself what the world would look like if you fixed them. That might involve changing business models, making other less customer-impacting sacrifices or simply challenging industry norms. The question for you and your team is whether there might be a significant pay-off from customers for being the first to take that pain-point away. If there would, then not only should you consider taking the action, you should also expect that if you don't, someone else will.

That's not always easy, of course. Changing your business model in a way that removes your historical competitive advantage is a very difficult thing for a management team to do, and even harder for a board and shareholders to support. I've seen at first hand how difficult it can be for a business to 'cannibalise itself' by leaping from a tried and tested business model or pricing model to one which is more open, more transparent but therefore almost certainly less profitable in the short term.

But there is one thing which is worse than cannibalising your own business model, and that's having someone else do it to you. In every market we've discussed there are new entrants with no such legacy to worry about, just itching to position themselves as the champion of the consumer and of fair and open dealing. Don't let them. We'll talk a bit later about how we can steel ourselves to reinvent our business models and become the masters and mistresses of our own destiny. There is a great potential pay-off from doing that.

That pay-off is a financial one as we find a way to build longer-term and more valuable relationships with customers who no longer feel slighted, marginalised or ripped off by our business practices. But potentially even more significant is the pay-off in terms of what we do to our brand and to our business reputation with consumers by being the first and the most visible of our competitors to challenge and change the model to put the customer first. We'll talk in the next chapter more about the reality that your business's reputation is now a bigger source of success (or failure) than it has ever been before.

The key to profiting from empowered customers

So what are we to do in this new reality where customers know much more about our costs and where commercial practices that give better deals to fickle customers and worse deals to loyal ones just won't wash anymore?

> You need to lead the change in your industry. To make yourselves the champions of clear and transparent commercial policies and to leave your competitors looking like the brands which are clinging on to 'how things used to be'.

But that's harder than it looks.

I was once asked to make a presentation to a financial services conference as a favour. My role was to be the 'outside observer' to provide them with a marketer's perspective on their industry. As luck would have it, just as I was beginning to wonder what I was going to say, the time came to renew my own house insurance. What an eye-opener. The conversation went something like this.

> **Me:** Last year you quoted me about £400 for house insurance. How much for this year?
>
> **Hapless insurance salesman:** That would be £1,200, sir.
>
> **Me:** What?? Nothing has happened this year that has led to me claiming on my insurance. Why on earth would you think you can triple my premium?
>
> **HIS:** Ah well, last year we also quoted you £1,200 but you then got a competitive quote for £400 which we price-matched. Do you have a competitive quote this time around?
>
> **Me (seeing where this is going but curious to see how badly this process is designed):** Why no, I don't, but we both know I can go and get one, so why not just give me your best quote now and save us all some time?
>
> **HIS:** I'm sorry, I can't do that. You need to call around our competitors and get another quote, and then call me back so I can match it.
>
> **Me:** So what you are telling me is that I have to go and get a better quote from your competitor. If I do that, what incentive have I got to ring you back at all?
>
> **HIS:** Err. . .

You can see where the story ends. I did end up with my house insured by someone else.

Telling this story to a room full of financial services executives was a fascinating experience. Far from unleashing a wave of denial or chasing me out of the room, they all nodded sadly and confirmed that my experience was typical and normal in many parts of their industry.

The pushback I got was simply to be asked how they could possibly get out of that situation. The reality, they explained to me, was that the maths was extremely clear. It was more profitable to offer good deals to new, disloyal or competitively active customers and, by extension, to offer worse deals to the most loyal customers.

In such a fiercely competitive market, someone was always going to be willing to offer an aggressive deal to take your best customers away from you and if you didn't respond you would lose that customer. A more equitable pricing strategy that offered the same deals to both loyal and new customers would simply mean that you were uncompetitive in the market for acquiring new customers and equally uncompetitive in the process of retaining customers who were being wooed by your competitors.

This is a financial bind which does not just happen in the insurance market. Retailers charging premium prices for warranties on consumer electronics, or for installation or delivery services are in the same pickle. Customers might think it unfair but if you stop charging premiums where you can, surely you reduce your ability to be competitive on core product pricing, which is exactly where pure-play new entrants are attacking you. Indeed, didn't we just spend some time on pricing, talking about how important it is to make margins where you can in order to compete?

Cinemas, theatre companies and concert promoters charging booking fees on top of basic ticket prices are in exactly the same position too. It might be obvious to everyone that charging an additional fee when someone buys a ticket online (often excruciatingly branded a 'convenience fee') is ridiculous, but try telling that to a board of directors who would see abandoning those charges as simply giving away money with little obvious payback.

So how do we resolve this dilemma? If the New Normal creates an environment where customers are increasingly aware of pricing, marketing and product availability practices that they regard as unfair, but those practices are important sources of our current profitability, what are we to do?

The answer comes in two parts. One involves going back to Economics 101, and the second involves something we will talk a lot about in this book – putting ourselves in the shoes of our customers.

The economics of doing the right thing

We have already discussed the fact that channel profitability is, for a modern retailer, the answer to the wrong question. In a world where customers shop through multiple channels, often for an individual purchase, it makes no sense to think about 'the internet channel' as being in some way less profitable than 'the retail channel', since neither can exist without the other. The right question for us to be asking is about the profitability of different customers, not of different sale channels.

We will take that thinking one step further. We need to move beyond thinking about the profitability of a customer for a specific transaction and instead think about the value of our relationship with our customers over the longer term.

On a particular day, I might buy a product from a retailer but then, getting it home, realise it isn't quite right for me and take it back later in the afternoon. Measured on that day, I'm not a particularly profitable customer. Indeed, the business might have lost money on me over the day if the product can't be easily resold or needs repackaging. A business can protect itself from my inconvenient behaviour with tougher returns policies, or cancellation charges if I've bought a subscription for something.

It's easy to see though, that the real value of my custom for that retailer isn't just measured on that one day. I might be a regular and valuable customer and indeed might have been for many years. The right way to deal with me in our thought experiment must be related somehow to the existence of that longer-term relationship.

A trainer I once knew used to illustrate this fact with the apocryphal story of the £9 pizza. A new employee in a pizza parlour gets into an argument with a customer who thinks that he has the wrong toppings on his pizza and refuses to refund him. The owner takes the new employee to one side and points out that that customer has been coming to the parlour every week since he was a little boy, and that the customer relationship that has just been sacrificed for the sake of £9 was actually worth tens of thousands.

Any good retailer knows this, which is why most would look after me when I tried to return my product even without knowing the long-term value of my business. Instinctively, they will take a hit on the day simply because of the chance that I will come back again and end up being a valuable customer. They will do the right thing for the long term at the expense of the short term.

Economically, we call this 'maximising customer lifetime value'. CLV is a simple concept. It measures the value of the business we do with a customer from the first sale we make with them to the last and recognises that a customer who makes small purchases but comes very frequently might be worth more than someone who makes a big purchase but only once. It also tells us that taking an action which encourages a customer to stay for longer can be just as profitable as taking an action that gets them to spend more on a particular day.

> **CLV is such a simple concept that every consumer business executive has heard it and used it a million times in meetings.**

We might be familiar with the term, but have we really thought it through? Because the principle of CLV contains within it the solution to our dilemma – what to do when, in the New Normal, customers can unpack our costs and margins, object to our uneven pricing policies and reject our hidden charges. Consider how we might break down the constituent parts of the CLV equation.

If your objective is to maximise the long-term value of your relationship with each customer, then the right action to take at any

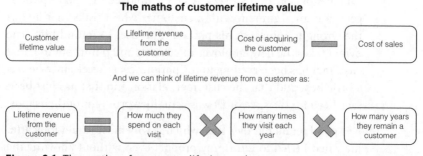

Figure 2.1 The maths of customer lifetime value

given point in time is self-evidently the one which supports that objective. If that means removing a hidden charge or reducing the price of a high-margin product then so be it. The long-term benefits will outweigh the short-term costs.

Won't they?

Well, only if we make the right decisions at the right time. Maximising CLV is not a blanket excuse to reduce every price or wipe out every source of short-term profit. If we make no profit in the short term, after all, then the long term will simply be the sum of a series of very small numbers.

> **As the economist John Maynard Keynes memorably said, in the long run we're all dead.**

Indeed, a weakness of the CLV approach to customer relationships is that the future is inherently unknown and therefore involves some risk. If I asked you to give me £10 today on the basis that I'd pay you back £15 in a month, your decision about whether to make the loan would certainly be impacted by whether or not you were worried that I'd skip town in the meantime.

Inevitably, therefore, there is an allure to profit today versus profit at some point in the future. Economists call this the discount rate – the time value of money – and it represents a sensible reason why we might not always chase future profits at the expense of today's.

Too many boardroom discussions about changing prices and policies that customers dislike but which drive current profit founder on this point. Those advocating change end up sounding like flowery do-gooders who just want to make the change because it is the right thing to do and any financial analysis supporting the change looks like it is promising jam tomorrow instead of jam today.

But there is a gritty reality to the concept of customer lifetime value. If you continue to charge that innocent-looking booking fee, penal cancellation charge or ridiculous warranty premium and the result is simply that customers choose to shop elsewhere, then it won't just be in the long term that your business is dead.

The resolution to those challenging boardroom discussions is to develop a viewpoint on what the consequences will be of not changing. Observing customer reaction to particular price points or commercial policies and spotting competitors or new entrants gearing up to change the industry norms are key to building this case.

And it is here that our analysis of the New Normal is so powerful. This rule of the New Normal is important not just because it is true but also because it is relatively new. Once upon a time, when consumers had less information at their fingertips, or when those transaction costs of sharing information were higher, our current commercial policies might have made sense, and might indeed have represented the strategy which maximised customer lifetime value. Certainly, the subscription business I described earlier could prove that rewarding customers who threatened to leave and penalising those who didn't was the most valuable strategy – not just in the short term, but over the long term too.

But the world has changed. And with it, so must our commercial policies. As we'll explore next, consumers have never had more ability to band together and campaign or complain about things they regard as unfair. And as technology changes have reduced the cost of entering many industries, it has never been easier for a new entrant to pounce on those complaints and position themselves as the champion of the consumer, stealing your business along the way.

The power of listening

If the first part of our response to a new empowered and informed customer base is to consider the lifetime value of each customer, the second is to listen to them actively and intelligently.

The warning sign that a historical commercial policy or source of profit is becoming an issue is of course best seen in the attitudes and behaviours of your current customers and those of your competitors. We'll talk later about some of the common techniques you can use to make sure that you and your team are genuinely immersed in customer feedback. An excellent starting point, however, in the New Normal, is to make sure you are properly listening online.

I had a conversation once with a casual dining brand. Before going to meet them, I spent a few weeks filtering Twitter and Facebook discussions that mentioned their brand and those of their most obvious competitors. What struck me more than anything else when we met was that their carefully crafted brand and market research packs bore no resemblance at all to what customers were saying about them when they spoke to each other online. There really is no substitute for immersing yourself in the raw chaos of social media discussions if you want to find out what people really think of you.

That is particularly true when a board is being asked to make decisions about commercial and pricing policies. With the best will in the world, the people sitting around most board tables do not live in the same world as their customers, least of all when it comes to money. I gave a presentation to the board of one brand I worked with, demonstrating the maths of what it is like to live on the average household income in the UK. What seemed like an academic debate about how much we should increase our monthly price was, for real people, a matter of whether they bought our product or gave their kids a summer holiday.

Actively listening to customers (and those who choose to be customers of your competitors) is therefore a critical tool to enable us to spot aspects of our products or pricing that we should think about changing. Our CLV-based business case is dramatically more powerful if we have evidence with which to support an analysis of how much we might lose in the long term if we try to support the short term despite what our customers want.

Action planning

How do you listen to customers? I've never met anyone in retailing who said they didn't care what customers thought, but the process of gathering customer feedback varies widely from business to business, as shown below:

- Do you spend enough time working in your own stores to actually chat to customers or deal with complaints (rather than the much more common royal visit where you do a shift and spend the rest of the year talking about that one visit to a store)?

▶

- Do you engage in focus groups or more interactive customer discussion sessions where issues can be vented and discussed in-depth?
- Do you do the same thing with customers of competitor brands to avoid the error of only listening to people who have chosen to do business with you?
- Do you read the comments on comment cards or customer feedback? Most executives I know will spend time reading the feedback summary report which gives the scores on the various questions that have been asked, but few will read the raw text of the 'any other comments' box, which is usually where all the useful data is.
- Do you listen in or take calls in your call centre?
- Do you respond personally to emails or social media-generated complaints?

A business where senior executives really know what's going on in the minds of customers, and those who choose to go to competitors, is self-evidently a much stronger one. How organised is your 'customer closeness' programme and how widely does it stretch across your management team?

Don't be like the CEO of one business who boasted that he knew what his customers were thinking because he talked to his chauffeur!

There is an additional benefit to getting to know what is in our customers' minds, and that is in understanding what pricing and commercial actions we might take that they might not like, but would regard as at least fair. Here lies the reconciliation between this rule and the last one.

For Rule 1, we discussed the importance of finding opportunities to price at a premium (or at least earn a margin) where we can in order to avoid being picked off by low-price competitors. However, we have now recognised that some of the historical margin opportunities that have supported our businesses are no longer acceptable to consumers in the New Normal. So how to tell the difference between an acceptable and an unacceptable pricing strategy?

The answer, of course, is with the consumer. While every consumer wants every product to be cheaper than it is, few would quibble with the idea that a differentiated, scarce and customised product should attract a premium over one that is none of those things. So the way to tell the difference between a clever forensic pricing strategy and an old-fashioned and unacceptable gouging of customers is to know your consumer well enough to predict how they will feel about a particular strategy and how they will react if you do it. That's an art, not a science, but we'll talk more in Part 2 about how we can prepare ourselves to do that well.

Bringing it together

You've seen that the New Normal has changed our sources of competitive advantage as customers have become better informed and more vocal as new entrants have sprung up to give our consumers new choices.

Our imperative is to respond to this changed world by changing ourselves and our consumer offerings. The key to that is to take a long-term view of the value of our relationship with each customer, sometimes sacrificing short-term profit to do so but always with an eye on the cost of the alternative. We want to cannibalise our own business rather than allowing others to do it to us.

This is a tough thing to do in the real world of quarterly earnings targets and short-term incentive plans. In Part 2 we will explore some tools that will allow us to build consensus where we need it in order to allow this kind of reinvention to happen.

In the meantime though, it is time to explore the next rule of the New Normal, and one we have mentioned several times already – that your brand reputation matters more than it ever did before and can make or break your business.

Chapter

3

Rule 3: Reputation will make or break a business

Think about the last time you went to a new restaurant for the first time. You might have been on holiday and trying out the local food, or it might have been a new restaurant in your home town that you were keen to check out. Either way, I know what you did before you went. You checked out the reviews, scores and recommendations on TripAdvisor or Yelp. You might even have had a look at the menu on one of those sites or the restaurant's own website and begun to think about what you might eat when you get there.

It seems almost extraordinary now that we once had to guess the relative merits of the eateries in our holiday destinations. We might have picked up a tip from the concierge in the hotel or by chatting to other guests, but beyond that, finding the best place to eat was an exercise in detective work, picking out the place with the nicest sign over the door, the cleanest looking linen tablecloths or the nicest-seeming staff.

Such a scattergun approach had both advantages and disadvantages. The disadvantages are obvious and many of us have a tale or two about shockingly bad meals in poor-quality restaurants that just happened to have nice napkins. The advantages, though, came in the surprise finds. The place you discover a couple of nights into your stay and then go to three more times just because it is so delightful.

If there are good and bad points about living in a world of online reviews for us customers, think about what it must be like for the restaurant owners.

> **When a string of two or three bad reviews can damage trading for weeks, you can't afford to let that happen.**

Equally, if poor reviews are damaging, terrific ones are tremendously valuable and worth seeking out. Self-evidently, this pressure to avoid bad reviews and encourage good ones has some positive effects. In the short term, restaurants will make every effort to do their best: to deliver your food order on time, make that food terrific and create for you an overall experience which is one you want to tell your friends about. No harm there. In the longer term, the businesses which fail to achieve that will, presumably, simply close and be replaced in a kind of free-market Darwinism by ones which do better. So, the result of online reviews making and breaking reputations should be good for everyone (except terrible restaurateurs).

But even the best operators will tell you that this world of perfect, free-flowing and freely available review scoring has its downsides too. Many have tales of wily customers effectively blackmailing them to avoid a bad review: "Give me a free dessert or I'll leave a one-star review."

When opening a new restaurant, it becomes so important to establish a high review score quickly that it is easy to imagine the team behind the business making sure that friends and family are recruited to do just that. It is also easy to imagine a clever restaurant team making sure to remind all those customers who seem to have had a nice time to leave a review online, but perhaps forgetting to say the same thing to those who had not.

And even failing businesses can develop tricks to get around their online reputation. One particularly terrible restaurant near me has changed its name twice in the last three years, I suspect solely for the purpose of jettisoning those past one-star assassinations.

If restaurants (and by close association hotels) offer a stark picture of how behaviours change when reputations are made and lost online in such a visible way, the same trends impact many other retail and hospitality sectors too. In the cinema industry at one point a few years ago, about 25% of customers bought their tickets online. However, if you changed the question and asked what percentage of ticket sales had involved the internet at all (to see what was on, read reviews of films and check out reviews of the venue itself) then the answer was closer to 100%. So even industries which don't appear to be massively driven by online sales can be impacted a lot by online reputation.

In fact, this is true even at the product level. There is a well-known phenomenon of television chefs mentioning an ingredient or a useful kitchen item, and sales of that product shooting up for a few weeks afterwards. The same thing is now true of online conversations. A discussion on Twitter, Facebook, Reddit or any number of other social media sites about, for example, the best brand of garden hose or the merits of different makers of men's shirts can have an immediate and measurable impact on sales of those products.

So here is our next rule of the New Normal: **Your brand reputation matters a whole lot more now than it ever did before**. It is heavily impacted by online discussion and that impact can have a huge effect on your sales and profitability.

Your brand, online

There are some things it is worth knowing about online brand reputation:

- It is very fluid. Reviewers are highly influenced by their own experience and unforgiving of what they see as errors. Surprisingly few online reviews are considered analyses of the pros and cons of your brand weighing up a final verdict. Most are either "this is brilliant" or "this was terrible" or some version of one or other of those.

- Time works in a funny way with online reviews. On the one hand, people tend to look at only the most recent reviews and not scroll back through pages of others, so the most recent reviews will weigh much higher. On the other hand, reviews never go away so if the most recent page of reviews includes some from a long time ago, they will still be impacting your business and reputation even now.

- As consumers, we have not yet properly worked out how to tell relevant reviews from irrelevant ones. We will tend to filter the reviews we read by ignoring ones where the reviewer is a complete idiot or can't spell, but beyond that it is very hard to tell whether this is a reviewer whose opinions might tend to match ours. As such, reviews from other consumers who live a long way away from us or whose needs were very different to ours can still influence us a lot.

- Consumers are very tribal with reviews, as they are with so many other things. A series of good reviews will tend to build up a momentum of their own as other customers become more likely to leave reviews that conform with the emerging pattern. Similarly, a series of bad reviews will tend to put reviewers into the mindset to think about what was wrong with their experience too.

- On the other hand, some people are contrarians and take delight in leaving a review which stands out from the herd. Equally, some of us are contrarians in the way we use reviews. I have a friend who always filters down to the terrible one-star reviews, even where those are a tiny minority of reviews for an otherwise terrific place. As a result, she often chooses not to visit places that might be delightful.

- Reviews will occasionally go viral, particularly if they are well written and funny. Unfortunately for business owners, reviews are most likely to be well written and funny when they are also scathing and critical, and it is usually those which get the most views.

These reviews of your brand and reputation often don't happen on review sites at all. In some industries, as with hotels and TripAdvisor, one online hub has become the de-facto default place to look.

> **For some industries, reputations are made and lost all over the online world.**

If I'm thinking about buying a particular brand of golf club or looking for a particular toy for my children, I'm as likely to find discussion, recommendations and feedback on LinkedIn as I am on Facebook. Indeed, many otherwise focused online communities for model aircraft enthusiasts, new parents or owners of a particular type of car will also have a 'general discussion' section that is full of people building or destroying your brand's reputation even though you aren't in any of those sectors.

Action planning

Google your own brand and spend some time reading what customers are saying about you. A simple search for your brand plus the word 'review' should bring up interesting answers, but you can have some fun narrowing your search down by adding 'terrible' or 'awful' as well.

The first page of search results is likely to be on major websites, but take the time to follow the search through to the later pages and find more obscure pockets of discussion. Narrowing your search by including terms like 'blog' or 'discussion' can also help.

There are two things to learn from the kind of online brand review I suggest you do above. The first, obviously, is to pay attention to what people are saying about you, both good and bad. This is not scientific or statistically valid feedback, but on the other hand it is a real and unfiltered look at how customers see you. This is incredibly valuable.

I once worked with a company whose internal reports about customer service levels were so abstract and massaged that the senior team had no idea that its call centre was near collapse – something that two minutes online made completely clear.

The second thing to learn from your online safari is about the kind of places your brand is being discussed. You'll never find every single reference, and wouldn't have the time to read them anyway, but if you find clusters or hubs where a lot of discussion happens (perhaps a hobbyist's forum dedicated to the products you sell) then you can both mark it for future reference and also consider having your social media team actually join in the discussion on your behalf.

A cautionary lesson from politics

The world of politics offers an interesting analogy here. Once upon a time, politicians addressed people through occasional and massively sycophantic interviews on television or radio where the great men (and they usually were men) were asked to share their thoughts with the rest of us. Messaging was controlled, relatively occasional, and generally very dull.

Well, that world has gone forever. A politician can now expect to have lots of opportunities to engage with a hungry 24-hour media in a way which is much less controlled and much less respectful but offers a more 'real' and interesting way to communicate. Even more importantly, the modern politician can engage directly with their consumer, the voter, through social media and other channels.

That is where politics has changed completely. As well as helping constituents, politicians have a much greater opportunity to establish their own personalities in the eyes of voters. They can be funny, rude, debate each other, get involved in consumer campaigns and generally become famous.

Indeed, we've now arrived at the point where, for many politicians, the direct online channel to voters is arguably more important than the traditional media. We've seen world leaders elected in countries around the world largely on the back of their Twitter count. That isn't necessarily always a good thing, but it is a truth. A part of the New Normal.

If that is true for politicians, it is true for brands and businesses too.

> **Many businesses still insist on trying to manage their brand and reputation using tools that look much more like the 1950s than the 21st century.**

A sombre group of Senior People gather in a boardroom somewhere to 'debate our brand values' with the help of an advertising agency. The marketing department is then sent forth to turn those brand values into this season's TV ad, which is then unveiled to an adoring and attentive public. Who promptly turn on Netflix and ignore the whole thing.

So what can we do to really build and manage a brand reputation in the New Normal? It can't be enough to just allow one to form out in the wild without reference to our business objectives or competitive strategy, so how can we influence and create a reputation in a world where no one wants to be lectured to?

Here are four lessons from the New Normal world of brand and reputation that every consumer business should embrace.

Start from the right place – a strong brand built on the truth of who you are

I've sat in too many of those Senior People discussions about brand and advertising for my own good. They often take a similar form. The agency provides some stimulus material to get the discussion going and a framework for the group to work through, and the discussion plods on from there.

At some point, all of those frameworks require a debate about 'our brand values', a set of (usually) single words or short phrases which are designed to encapsulate perfectly what Bob's Storage Company really stands for. The discussion is usually just about as excruciating as you'd imagine, and after a while the debate wears away any actually interesting ideas, which is why so many lists of brand values include things like 'fun', 'innovation' and 'trustworthiness' because they are just too obvious and bland for anyone to really object to. They are the last adjectives standing in the brand development game of musical chairs.

The result of that process, though, is that there is something missing: the truth.

I once worked in a business which had a reputation that we could politely describe as 'commercial'. We were a successful business, put our prices up regularly, took full advantage of any strong market position and as a result made a lot of money. In the middle of one particularly angst-ridden senior people discussion about branding (I think someone was describing us as an egg, with a strong protective shell), I suggested that it might be important to start our brand development from what people actually thought of us. We might not want 'greedy gits' as a brand value, but it should be important at least to acknowledge our starting point in our customers' minds.

I might as well have spat on the floor. No one wanted to hear about what our actual customers thought, the debate continued and we ended up with our own unique combination of fun, innovation and trustworthiness. And also went on to make some spectacularly unmemorable ads as a result.

> **The truth is that your brand is not just what you wish it to be.**

What you want your brand to be is in some ways the least important part of the equation. Unless you are an entirely new business that no one has heard of, your brand already exists as the sum of the impressions that your customers and potential customers have about you.

There's a saying that your brand is what people say about you when you aren't there. That has never been more true than in the New Normal where the internet has created a whole lot more rooms that you aren't in, and given people the ability to praise you, complain about you and campaign for or against you in ways they never had before. It would seem a good idea therefore to eavesdrop a bit on those conversations.

You can do that with market research of various kinds, and it is a good discipline to do so. Find an agency that doesn't look afraid to tell you the truth, make sure they are asking the right people what they think and listen to the answer.

But one terrific aspect of the New Normal is that you can eavesdrop on discussions about your brand – right now, online. If you are pausing to do our action planning exercises, then you've already done that once.

In Part 2 we'll talk about some of the essential skills of the New Normal and high on the list is the ability to dig around online to gather information. Indeed, this is one of the defining differences between the lives of kids who are being brought up in the New Normal from the generations which preceded them. If you have access to all the knowledge in the world at your fingertips, the skill is not in gathering data, it's in filtering it and finding the important stuff.

For now, suffice it to say that finding those discussions and being brave enough to listen to them raw and unfiltered is a key part of brand development in the New Normal.

That's not to say that all the negative things you'll hear about your brand have to become brand values.

> **"Buy from us, our customer service is terrible" is not a winning line. "Buy from us, our customer service is brilliant" isn't a winning line either if everyone knows it isn't true.**

A brand rooted in falsehoods lets everyone down. You've wasted your advertising budget, your customers think less of you and your front-line teams in store and elsewhere are embarrassed every time they see the ads.

So the first step in building a strong brand reputation online is listening to your customers and finding out what they think of you right now. But what do you do with that information when you've got it?

Two things. First, if you hear negative things about your brand that are important and brand-damaging, why not fix them? Indeed, this is real brand development. Listening to customers, triaging their concerns and addressing them through your business strategy is much more likely to grow your bottom line than just making ads about how fun and innovative you are.

You don't have to fix everything, and indeed you probably can't, but profound strategy development can come from listening to what people associate with your brand and then doing something about it. Customers might feel that your brand has some positive attributes that they really value but which they don't see brought to life in store. That in turn can become an amazing trigger for your people-development strategy.

If customers think your brand should be exciting and energetic but find the experience in your store boring and lacklustre, then you are doing something wrong in failing to create an environment in which your colleagues can bring the brand to life. Later in Part 2 we'll explore how to engage your front-line teams in the whole strategy for the business. Helping them bring your brand to life is the most important part of that.

The second thing you can do with real customer feedback about your brand is reflect it in the brand values you choose to align the business around. People think your brand is quirky and original? Lean into it. People see your business as cheaper than your rivals? Lean into that too, with a brand campaign that makes clear you will do whatever you can to keep prices low.

But whatever you do, don't ignore the reality of where you start in your customers' minds. That can only lead to inauthentic and wasted communication.

Authenticity trumps consistency – be true to who you are

Authentic is a funny word, isn't it? Some of the best known and best loved retail and consumer brands have strong brand recognition because of something we instinctively call authenticity. There is a clear personality to the brand, and it shines through whenever and however we interact with the business.

Often, that's because there is actually a strong personality behind the brand. Many founder-led or family-owned businesses are able to achieve this. Delivering a clear point of view through their actions and marketing communications because that point of view is the one that is really held by those behind the business. UK retail phenomenon Lush demonstrates this well. Lush is a business selling soaps, cosmetics and other beauty products to a young, savvy and politically active customer base. Its retail execution is fantastic with vibrant, strongly perfumed stores full of colleagues drawn very much from the target market, with loads of product demonstrations and other interactivity going on all day.

The business also has a strong campaigning heritage. Not just with campaigns related to the product set (against animal testing, for instance), but for a whole variety of other causes that are important to their customers – the protection of wildlife, against climate change, in favour of immigration and more.

Both the clarity of the retail execution and the consistency of the campaigning effort are often attributed to the fact that the business is led by its founders, and often reflects their beliefs in its campaigns.

But you don't have to be a founder-owned business to have a strong brand point of view and live it consistently. Ryanair's cheeky "If you don't like it, don't buy it" attitude to low-frills airline travel may have been strongly influenced by its CEO, but he doesn't own the business.

> **What does create authenticity is a strong point of view, clearly and passionately expressed.**

Expressing authenticity is harder than it looks. Business leaders are surrounded by people trying to smooth out, dumb down or hedge any expression of opinion. For fear of offending someone, attracting bad headlines or on the grounds that they might get sued, businesses end up coating messages in caveats, exemptions, small print and other nonsense.

But the reality of the New Normal is that everyone sees through that, and writes your business off as just another faceless corporate bureaucracy. It's personality that stands out, and customers end up being remarkably forgiving of a clearly expressed opinion even if they don't necessarily agree with it.

I once worked in a subscription-based business that put its prices up most years. Generations of management had decreed that the best way to fulfil our legal obligation to inform customers of the price increases was to write the longest, most boring and most complicated letter possible, burying the price change in the second-to-last paragraph, which direct marketers know is the one fewest people will actually read. No wonder we had that 'greedy gits' brand value.

As an experiment, one year we took the opposite tack, writing a clear and concise letter which opened with the news about pricing and then, in a few sentences, outlined why we had done what we'd done. Surprise surprise, the reaction from customers was no worse than when the message was hidden, and our own teams had a much easier job justifying the change.

I had a similar experience with the positive power of a clearly expressed message when I ran a retail business. An outraged customer began an email exchange with me. He had a genuine grievance about a promotional offer that had been badly worded, but he was also extremely rude about it, including some very aggressive phone calls with some of our head office team.

In the end, I told him to get lost. I thought he had a fair point in his original complaint and we had tried our best to make things right but that was no excuse at all for his behaviour and I didn't want him in any of our stores. He was, needless to say, outraged and immediately tried to checkmate me by posting our private email exchange all over Facebook. Our teams, though, were delighted to find that customers online unanimously agreed with the stance we'd taken, and thought we were entirely responsible in protecting our own colleagues in store from his abuse.

> **It would have been very easy to write a 'we apologise for any inconvenience caused' kind of letter to try to brush an incident under the carpet, but it turned out that having an opinion and voicing it was a much better route.**

Action planning

What does your business stand for? Inauthentic brands are all around us. The innovative company that hasn't launched a new product in ages. The fun and personable business that still has acres of small print.

Well, the bad news is that if that is true for others, it may well be true for the brand you work for too. With your team, discuss the following questions:

- Are we clear about what we stand for? (If not, you might need to have one of those senior people brand debates, and you have my sympathy.)
- How would our customers know what we stand for?
- If the answer is that we tell them in our advertising, that's not good enough. What do we do that would cause them to draw their own conclusions about our brand and come up with the same answer we have?
- *Equally, what do we do that isn't consistent with the brand values we espouse?*

Finally, have a discussion about what I think is the most powerful strategy formulation question of all: If these are our brand values, what would we <u>never</u> do?

This last one is a killer. If you and your teams are clear about the red lines your brands create and the actions you would never countenance as a business because of who you are, then you probably not only have a brand positioning, but are actually presenting it to the outside world.

In practice, management teams often conflate authentic with consistent. Their reasoning is that if we want to have one opinion, one tone of voice in all of our communications then surely we'd better make them all exactly the same.

This is a big mistake. Consistency comes from layers of checks and approvals, which is the opposite of authentic. A too-many-cooks approach to communicating with customers is a bit like the senior people brand meeting. Everything interesting or funny gets objected to by someone, and what comes out of the end of the process is bland and vanilla.

If two passionate advocates of your brand end up slightly contradicting each other, customers will understand if the two points are obviously coming from the same place. That's no excuse for factual messages about products or customer service being contradictory (in fact, we have a whole chapter on the danger of that coming up), but having multiple voices expressing your brand values in their own way is a positive, not a negative.

People make reputations, not processes – find your brand ambassadors and set them free

Voices are exactly what you need to express your brand, and as a consumer business you already have plenty of them. The trick is to find, nurture and empower them.

Iconic British retail brand HMV, sellers of music and DVDs, was in difficulty and drifting towards going bust, and was having to make lots of people in its head office redundant as a result. A horrible time for everyone involved.

Unfortunately, tragedy for HMV drifted towards comedy when it sat down with its social media team to make them redundant. It hadn't occurred to the senior directors in the room that it might be sensible to take back control of the log-ins to the brand's various social media accounts before firing the people who used them. The predictable result was that the social media team live-tweeted their own redundancies to the horror of the senior executives and the morbid hilarity of millions observing online.

A couple of weeks later I was interviewed by a retail trade journal about this event and what I thought it meant for big businesses. Surely, the interviewer asked, brands should take back control of their social media presences and insist on lawyers approving any post before it went online. After all, the argument went, by delegating to social media managers these brands were putting their reputations into the hands of '25-year-old junior marketeers' (I quote).

My response was simple. Any retail business worried about putting its reputation into the hands of young and junior employees was already in big trouble, because the millions of people who walked into its stores every week were being served by exactly that kind of employee, and were forming their impression of the brand based on those interactions.

> **If you want young colleagues to represent your brand really well, then it would seem like a good idea to make them enthusiastic, well informed and passionate advocates of that brand.**

If you don't want young people to tell others that you are treating them badly, an excellent start would be to not treat them badly in the first place.

Hopefully live-tweeting internal meetings is not a problem you'll have all that often, but the story illustrates a broader point. Not only is it important to empower those people controlling your social media accounts to represent your brand with passion and enthusiasm, but it is equally important in a consumer business to empower all your people in the same way.

Here's an important three-stage thought experiment:

1. Imagine standing at a podium in front of a large crowd of your customers, telling them things about yourself. You have the only microphone, you are standing on an elevated stage. You can see the audience, but not particularly well past all of the lights. You are broadcasting, and that's how marketing communications felt in the last century. Of course, there is still some audience interaction. If you make people laugh, it is apparent and if you say something particularly awful you will hear the murmurs and hisses coming back at you. But you are still fundamentally in a one-way world, with control of the message you deliver.

2. Now, by comparison, imagine sitting at a table with a focus group of your customers. There are eight or ten of them around the

table with you and you can all see each other and there are some drinks and snacks on the table. Now the process of communicating about your brand is very different. People will interrupt you to disagree with things you say which they don't agree with. They will also echo and amplify things you say that they do agree with. After a while, they will start to talk to each other too, with the advocates around the table leaping to your defence and the more hostile in the group bringing up their anecdotes of things your business has done to upset them. You are a contributor to the discussion, of course, and you have some authority and credibility as the representative of your brand, but you are no longer broadcasting. You are debating, advocating, persuading and interacting. As the New Normal emerged, marketing evolved from the first analogy to this one.

3. But now take that analogy further and imagine that of the ten people around the table, two of them are front-line employees of yours. They too will interact in the conversation. They will defend your brand if they feel inclined to do so, will sometimes agree with criticisms of your business and will have their own take on your strategies and objectives. Sometimes as the discussion flows around the table it will be between your customers and these employees. You have a chance to intervene too, but it will be obvious after a while that the customers in the group regard these two employees as just as much representatives of your business and brand as you are.

That last scenario is how marketing works today. You can create messages, of course. But once that work is done, you are going to take it into an interactive, chaotic and noisy discussion with your customers and every one of your employees who talks to customers will be there around the table, often supporting your messages, but definitely with their own perspective and input too.

So how on earth can you make sure that the outcome of all this discussion is that customers like and admire your brand, want to be associated with your business, and want to buy your products?

Here are some practical steps you can take:

- Once you have a brand position that you are comfortable you can project with integrity, it is critical to recruit your staff as ambassadors for it. And that means all of them – store staff, delivery drivers, sales people, call centre workers, service engineers. Everyone.

- It is not sufficient that everyone in your organisation knows what the business is trying to say about itself. They have to agree with the message. That either means changing the message until it is one that your teams believe, or changing what you do in order to demonstrate that you mean what you say. If you present to the world a brand based on the expertise and skill of your people but at the same time they see you slashing the training budget, the message will not stick either with them or your customers.

- In fact, it is a terrific idea not just to brainstorm a brand with an agency and then try to convince your people to advocate it. Many great businesses are now doing it the other way around – finding ways to co-create the brand with people from all around the business, creating an outcome which is much more authentic as a result. One hospitality brand I worked with did this simultaneously across multiple European territories, not only creating a great brand statement but creating an alignment around it which crossed borders and language barriers.

Take risks, live in the moment and apologise quickly when you get it wrong

Developing and nurturing a brand reputation in the New Normal is risky. A casual remark from a disaffected colleague can disappoint and drive away a customer. A careless or thoughtless tweet can create a ferocious and campaigning reaction from angry readers. The sheer relentless pace of an always-on digital world can mean that standards drop. Messages get less scrutiny, silly mistakes creep in and trolling attacks from anonymous internet accounts get more attention and response than they deserve.

But all those risks are manageable with experience and with the right resourcing. It's a tough call to invest time and resource in building brand 'dialogue' with customers. That's particularly true through social media where a direct relationship between activity and sales is often hard to prove.

But when your brand is so important, and the potential number of people you can influence is so large, investing is not optional.

I've seen too many retail businesses balk at hiring a second or third social media manager while still signing off television ad campaigns costing millions of pounds which are likely to influence fewer people.

Far from being an area you can penny-pinch in, social media is likely to be the next domain of the rock-star marketer. It is already possible to see in the UK and US that a small number of brands are benefiting disproportionately from having one or more really terrific social media managers who have the knack of getting the brand across in a way that people like, respond to and retweet.

Some of those social media stars have already been poached from one brand to another and I'm sure that will happen more. Cutting through the noise online with your brand is difficult, and if you find a team who can do it you should keep them.

As we've seen already, investing in brand communication is not just about investing in the team who operate your digital channels. A modern consumer business is represented every day by thousands of colleagues in stores and outlets around the world. No surprise, then, that a growing part of the management activity in the most successful brands is devoted to co-creating the brand with colleagues, sharing the brand message widely around the business and making policy changes that empower colleagues to really deliver for customers. In this sense, the HR and training teams are now more important to your brand journey than (whisper it) the marketing department.

Bringing it together

So, the New Normal has changed the way we should build and grow our brand and business reputation, and has made it much more critical that we do so. When positive (and negative) stories about your brand can be catapulted around the internet in minutes and seen by millions it matters more than it ever has that you and all of your colleagues are active creators of, and advocates for, your brand.

In Part 2 we will explore some of the tools and knowledge necessary to do that. First, though, let's consider another reality of the New Normal, one which has particularly big implications for retailers – the way the role of the store has changed forever.

Chapter

Rule 4: Location matters, but for different reasons than it used to

I can't remember the exact number which was the last straw for me but I think it was £2.80. £2.80 for a bag of sweets at a motorway service station. I'm not even sure if I can remember which sweets, though let's face it, it was probably Minstrels.

What I do remember is being so shocked by the price that I left without buying anything and spent the rest of my journey along the motorway brooding about pricing strategy.

It wouldn't be fair just to pick on WH Smith, the stationer and provider of expensive sweets at service stations and public transport outlets. They are in good company. Quite often the coffee you buy from the chain of coffee shops, the lunch you buy from the snack bar and many of the other products on sale in airports, railway stations and other travel hubs are more expensive than they would be on the high street.

As we explored in Rule 1, there is a good and obvious reason for that. By and large, when you are in those places you are in a hurry, and don't have a lot of choices of other places to buy the thing you want to buy. From that perfect storm – customers with time pressure and limited competition – comes the inevitable result. Higher prices.

I might not have bought my chocolate, but plenty of travellers do and so it makes sense to take the margin opportunity where you find it.

The power of place

As well as being an example of pricing strategy in action, my service station pricing experience illustrates another key aspect of strategy for any retailer, and that is the value of place, of being there, and having products to sell at the exact time and in the exact place where the consumer finds themselves when they need those products.

Place has a long history in marketing theory. Indeed, it is one of the famous 4 Ps alongside product, price and promotion.

> **In traditional marketing theory, place had value because buying things was, for the consumer, a fairly expensive thing to do.**

Buying things was not necessarily expensive financially, but it was in terms of the time and effort required to go from one potential vendor to another.

Recall the example from the introduction of buying a fridge. Once upon a time that often meant wandering from store to store writing down model numbers and prices. That might mean driving or getting the bus from one retail park to another and the whole exercise was so difficult that in the end most people ended up only checking one or two places and then buying from one of those. The same was true in non-retail businesses. Yes, we know that before hiring a builder to do some work we should get three or four competing quotes but for many people the hassle of finding that many competitors and then arranging to be at home that many times is just too much.

All of those barriers to shopping around take us back to those 'transaction costs' we discovered in Rule 2, the financial and non-financial penalties that we face every time we try to get another quote or visit another retailer. In a world where transaction costs are relatively high, customers will not shop around that much. And when that is true, to quote Woody Allen: "Showing up is 80% of life."

If you, as a retailer, make sure that you have stores in all the places where customers might want to shop, you can win that lovely high-margin business from those who stumble over you, but can't be bothered to seek out your competitor.

In that high transaction cost world, businesses placed great importance on what they called 'distribution strategy', making sure that their products, services or retail stores were as visible and easily accessible to consumers as possible. If you could win the distribution game, you'd ultimately win the sale.

For retailers, that often meant having as many stores as possible in as many places as possible. This psychology became very deeply entrenched for executives who grew up in the retail space, and even to this day a lot of retail financial results commentary is rooted in how many stores you have.

At its wildest excess, the result of this focus on distribution was retail businesses which had several stores in the same town, often only a few doors apart. The obvious inefficiency of paying rent and salaries on several stores in the same market was outweighed by the deep-seated fear of missing out on a sale from a customer who might walk past one store but not get as far as the other.

Place in the New Normal

This concept of distribution strategy is obviously still very important. It is also easy to see how it has changed beyond recognition in a world of instant online research. Indeed, as we've already seen in our rules of the New Normal, if products can easily be listed online for near cost price, and if everyone has instant access to those listings through a simple Google search for a product or brand, then the transaction costs faced by consumers have dropped massively.

Not only does a search for fridges online deliver tens of millions of results, but even the first couple of pages present dozens of retailers and manufacturers, all competing on price. No need to get the bus anywhere to do price comparison now.

If transaction costs are much lower in the New Normal, then the right distribution strategy for your brand has probably changed too.

Certainly, the balance between online presence and physical retail distribution on the high street or retail park has changed. If customers don't need to shop around, and can easily find you online, then it is harder to justify the endless chase towards having an outlet (or two) on every possible street.

Considering how profound this change has been in the last decade, it is amazing how many retailers still cling to the distribution strategies of a different era. Read retailer's financial results presentations and the press coverage that they generate and you will see that they often lead with a statement about how many new shops they have opened.

Indeed, the main performance measure used when talking about retailers (same store like-for-like sales growth) is a fascinating glimpse into the psychology of an industry undergoing more change than it can cope with.

By putting store sales front and centre and relegating online sales to an after-thought, the metric is an essentially backward-looking glimpse of days gone by.

And yet, for all that change, our high streets are still full of shops that trade profitably. Major consumer brands still regard physical distribution of product to consumers as a massively important channel to market.

Clearly, even if the rules of the game have changed, there is still value in being in the right place at the right time. Indeed, in a world where there is so much pressure to sell product lines at cost or less, finding the precious opportunity to actually earn a profit margin is more important than ever before.

> **If distribution strategy was once a race to be everywhere you could, in the New Normal the right answer is a bit more subtle.**

For a start, it will vary depending on the kind of product you are selling. If it is one where models are fairly standard and prices and performances can easily be compared across brands and through the web, then the value of location will be lower (those fridges, again). However, if your product or brand are in some way unique or hard to compare with others (fashion, for example) then some of the old value of being where customers are is still there. It is no accident that while electronics, video games, books and music have faded away from our high streets, clothing retailers have remained there.

Equally, if you make or sell a product which can be easily delivered to home, then you'd better go ahead and do that – and that changes your distribution strategy a lot too. One of the biggest long-term challenges facing supermarkets is not competition from low-cost competitors, but the fact that so much of their capital is invested in huge edge-of-town hypermarkets. Those are the places we used to go to stock up each week on bulky and heavy shopping that we could load into the car and drive home. Now that we can have all of that stuff delivered to us, the economics of the hypermarket have changed entirely, and the decisions made decades ago to buy long leases and build huge buildings no longer look quite so smart.

On the other hand, if your product is one that does not lend itself quite so well to internet delivery, then retail distribution might still be a money spinner. Again, some categories like shoes and clothes have weathered the internet storm better than others because of a desire to see and touch products before consumers buy. Other categories have survived on the high street because the products they sell are too small or too perishable to deliver to home or because they are products that consumers want to consume when they buy them, without waiting.

Action planning

How have transaction costs changed in your industry over the last ten years, and what does that mean for your physical store estate?

Before you answer that, be aware of a trap in that question. When we build a store estate we are not only making financial investments. We are also building an organisation around those stores and that organisation has feelings and values of its own.

▶

In that context, it is hard to answer the question of how many stores you need in the New Normal without ending up justifying the estate you already have. No one wants to admit that a ten-year lease signed three years ago might not be an asset in the new economy. But that doesn't stop it from being true.

So in thinking about how many stores you need (and where) you need to start by thinking about the role those stores play in your relationship with your customer. Which of the archetypes we laid out above apply to you? Are you selling products bought by people who need them right now or products that people don't buy online? Or are you selling products that people can perfectly easily buy online but where you believe that great physical displays can encourage additional sales?

A powerful technique when asking this question is not to start from where you are now, but to ask yourself what store estate you would build today if you were starting with none. That's the optimal answer. The challenge then is to get there from where you are today.

The real lesson from the bag of sweets

And that brings us back to my Minstrels. I said earlier that I wouldn't pick on WH Smith, but they are a fascinating business that is worth a closer look. For many years, both on the high street and in their transport-related travel stores they have followed a range of strategies that have made management theorists twitch in horror. They have ruthlessly dropped product categories that weren't performing, have raised prices consistently and aggressively, have invested next to nothing in loyalty, databases or other sexy marketing technologies and operate stores which, let's be candid, could do with some investment.

All of those things sound like a recipe for losing customers and destroying a business. And yet, despite all forecasts to the contrary, the business has done consistently well. It has grown sales in its travel outlets and, while it has lost some sales on the high street, it has driven profit growth, which makes it the envy of the retail sector.

> **WH Smith became the envy of the retail sector by developing an early and highly perceptive insight into the changed role of 'place' in the New Normal.**

The categories WH Smith has dropped are largely those where price comparison with the internet is easy, and where a high street chain was always going to lose out. The products it continues to sell are those that are either hard to compare with others or are products, such as magazines and newspapers, which people buy because they want them now, not later. And it has pushed prices up, but also deployed a bewildering array of multi-buy, 3 for 2 and other promotions which help to take the sting out of high individual prices.

And in doing all of those things, it has developed a distribution strategy which is fit for the New Normal. It has invested heavily in growing its travel business, where by definition it earns itself a small local monopoly by being the only outlet in the station, and that lack of investment in the high street business has helped it remain the last major newsagent chain standing, meaning again that it often ends up with a de facto monopoly on a high street for the products that it sells.

Against all the odds, a really smart reading of the new world, and a focused and determined distribution strategy built in response to that, have made the business a long-term winner.

Distribution strategy in the New Normal

None of that is to say that the right distribution strategy for all businesses is to try to mimic WH Smith. The right strategy for a given retailer, or a given brand, depends on the kind of factors we've discussed. The right strategy for your business might be:

- Entirely online. Unburdened by the cost of physical distribution, you can focus on standing out in those all-important Google searches.
- A small number of very high-end physical outlets that act as brand amplifiers and creators of loyal customers. Think about

those amazing Apple stores and the role they play in building that brand.

- Physical distribution chosen very carefully to make sure you are there when customers need you.

Sun Tzu has to be the most quoted, most clichéd and yet least understood of all the business or military 'strategy thinkers'. That's hardly surprising. Few of us are running rampaging armies, and few of us can read the great man's thoughts in the language they were written in. Translated from ancient Chinese into English, many of the aphorisms and sayings have become banal. Even taking that risk, however, the writings in the Art of War can be quite thought-provoking if you give them time and space. Here's one of my favourites: "Know yourself, and you will win all battles."

I'm sure there is a profound underlying philosophical and military interpretation of that quote, but I favour a more direct one. As businesses faced with the changing world of the New Normal, it is easy to become mesmerised by the apparent strengths of new entrants into our markets, and in turn to regard the differences between their businesses and ours as our weaknesses and 'legacy problems'.

We marvel at the low-cost base that a pure-play online competitor has. It hasn't had to invest in leases for properties for sales and service outlets. In turn, it hasn't had to hire loads of staff to populate those properties and talk to customers. It often has processes, systems and approaches which are more efficient and less costly than ours because they are new and shiny.

Sometimes, when we allow ourselves to envy our new competitors, we are right to do so. As we'll see in examples throughout this book, many established businesses have allowed themselves to try unthinkingly to 'protect' their historical assets and have missed the emergence of whole new markets as a result. It is foolish to look at new approaches and dismiss them without really considering how customers will feel about them, and doubly foolish to allow the sunk cost fallacy to force us to try to offer a sub-standard, unchanging, costly service to our customers when more nimble competitors will simply compete us out of existence.

> **Before we dismiss the old out of hand in our search for the new, we should take the time to properly audit what we have that our competitors don't and how those assets can be put to good use for our customers and our shareholders.**

We have talked about the importance of really listening to what customers actually think of our business, and in Part 2 we'll explore some practical ways to do that. Given the right research programme, one of the things we can begin to understand is what the key underlying drivers of a positive brand reputation are for our business.

Imagine running some kind of brand satisfaction survey (we'll talk about the best of these in Part 2), but also asking some more specific questions about the experience your customers have with your business (how easy it is to find your products, how enjoyable your store experience is, how knowledgeable your sales teams are). Given enough data, it is then fairly straightforward to build a model showing the relationships between these scores. Which are the aspects of your end-to-end customer experience that really drive your reputation and underpin high customer satisfaction?

If you do that, you'll find that many of the things that really differentiate brand experiences for retailers are people-related and are about the interactions they have with your brand in store.

I've built this correlation model in three different industries and found one remarkably consistent answer. One of the top two or three drivers of overall brand appreciation has always been whether or not customers feel like someone says hello to them when they walk into the store. That's not, of course, because we want some robotic greeting parroted to us when we are shopping.

> **The kind of store estate populated with colleagues who look up, smile, nod and say hello to customers is probably doing lots of other things right too and feels to customers like a place they want to be.**

It's not rocket science to recommend that we discover what our customers like and then do more of it, but it is still surprisingly rare to observe this strategy in the wild.

So by understanding the drivers of brand appreciation, and also by thinking about the different aspects of services that consumers are willing to pay for at different times (see Rule 1), we can begin to think differently about the role of the physical store in our business.

Six reasons to have a store

Why have a store at all in this multi-channel world? Here are six reasons, and I'm sure you can come up with more:

1. **Convenience**: If your market happens to be one of those where convenience is important – when a customer who wants your product really wants it here and now – the retail distribution you have is an obvious advantage over a pure-play competitor.

2. **Discovery**: Yours might not be a product or service that people know they want until they stumble over it. Many businesses selling luxury goods, knick-knacks and non-essential homewares would be examples of this phenomenon. A customer may love that throw cushion, but may not have thought to type the words into a search engine.

3. **Product experience**: Some products simply sell better when we can see, touch, smell and generally experience them first. Few people would buy a car without at least sitting in it first, but even for smaller products there can be a great advantage to putting them on display. An art business I worked with found it very easy to sell pictures in a gallery environment but almost impossible online when the real beauty of the images and the quality of the printwork was harder for customers to discern.

4. **Curation**: I might know generally the kind of product I want, but find it easier to narrow down a choice when I can see several examples of the product laid out together.

5. **Linked sales**: Customers for product A might be much more likely to also buy product B if they seem them displayed and promoted together. If I'm buying a travel book, might I want a map too? Many online sellers famously push addition sales through the

'People who bought this product also bought that one' approach but a physical product display can do this in a much richer way.

6. **Active selling**: With physical product distribution comes the ability to have a salesperson on hand to answer questions, point out features and, at the right time, close the sale. For many categories of product, and particularly for more expensive products, this can generate valuable incremental revenue over and above just hoping people click 'Buy'.

With all those advantages, it is a wonder that businesses selling goods and services to consumers don't all line up to open stores, isn't it? Interestingly, there is an increasing trend for exactly that to happen. Web giants are exploring physical distribution, often through pop-up or short-term stores but increasingly also by investing in (or buying up) store businesses. Amazon's purchase of Whole Foods and its continuing experiments in other types of retail store is only the most visible example.

Brand owners too can see the advantages. The iPhone might be an amazing product, but it would not be where it is today without the network of Apple stores and also the third-party mobile phone stores the brand has partnered with around the world.

That is not to say, however, that the advantages of having a physical store estate are in some way automatic or inevitable. It might be the case that a chain of retail stores would be an asset that a web-only new entrant would envy. That does not mean that a bloated, untidy, boring and undifferentiated retail chain full of employees who wish they weren't there is going to do you any good at all.

There is much to be said about the process of reinventing a legacy business so that the 'asset' aspect of it outweighs the 'liability' aspect. Here are some key points to bear in mind:

- We need to be clear about which of the potential advantages we are trying to capitalise on, and then be ruthlessly focused on ensuring that we bring them to life.
- If 'active selling' is going to be our competitive advantage we need our stores to be populated with personable, well-trained and effective sales people, and plenty of them.
- If we are going to make sales because we showcase beautiful products in a terrific environment that allows people to

discover them and generates the desire to buy, we need to make sure our shops are fitted out to achieve that, and don't resemble an untidy jumble sale.

- We need to make sure that in seeking the advantages of physical retail sales, we don't give up on the advantages of selling online. The smart reader of Sun Tzu will appreciate that the idea is to have the best of both worlds by having a terrific, cost-effective online operation, strong physical distribution, as well as creating new services that combine the best of both, like 'click and collect'.

- We need to carefully mitigate the disadvantages of our legacy operations (which are usually the costs of sales and service channels and the inflexibility which comes with older IT systems), but without losing the potential benefits they give us. Too many organisations have decided to keep their customer service operations, but then tried so hard to reduce the cost of those operations through outsourcing and the layering of automated menus that they end up being a pain-point for customers rather than an asset.

Avoid rediscovering the past

There is, then, a powerful exercise for a leadership team of a business challenged by the New Normal to undertake. By really understanding what delights customers, and then carefully reviewing the different activities which our business undertakes and considering how they can contribute to that delight, we can find the all-important areas where our historical market position and scale represents an advantage rather than a disadvantage.

By combining an energetic drive into the 'new' (building the new channels and creating the new product versions that our new-entrant competitors are doing) with a shrewd leveraging of the 'old' where it is helpful to our customers, we can deliver extraordinary results.

As powerful as this exercise is, it is a dangerous one too. It is human nature to regard the thing we are working on right now as important, and the business we have built over time as valuable. Time and again I have seen businesses review their current operations through the lens of "Can we think of a justification for continuing to do this?" rather than "Does this drive a great customer experience?" There is always a reason for continuing a business activity or thinking about it for a bit longer, but this approach is complacent and woolly, and is precisely the one which leads a business to try to defend its historic operations while being systematically outcompeted by new entrants.

A 'zero-based' and bold approach is required if we are to really unpick what actually matters to our customers. To use an analogy from a different industry, I once worked with a mobile company that challenged itself to figure out the 'right' amount of investment to make in its call centre customer service operation for the cheaper 'pay as you go' mobile business. Reams of analysis was done on average call times, call volumes and efficiency opportunities. A long list was produced of ways to automate certain call types or encourage customers to use the web instead.

That was true, of course, but it represented the 'how do I start from here' approach to business review. A better question was why any customer should need to call a call centre about a pay-as-you-go mobile phone at all? When we started to think about the problem more broadly, we realised that if a customer could not connect their phone to their router in order to go online and watch Netflix, there was no call centre they could ring at Netflix, Google or the router company. Only we, the mobile business, operated a call centre to try to help with that problem. So why do that at all? Why not simply have some instruction manuals accessible online and leave these customers (who were not paying a monthly subscription) to fend for themselves?

Once we challenged ourselves with that scary question, the task became much easier. It turned out that there were good reasons to be there for our customers. We wanted to be an important and useful brand in their communications lives. We wanted, ultimately, to have such a good relationship with them that we could sell them additional services like subscription mobile, home broadband and other things. Precisely by being the only element in the chain which could offer any help, we believed we could differentiate ourselves.

Realising that was why we wanted to offer customer service made designing and optimising that service much easier. Rather than making it harder and harder to call a call centre to ask basic questions about billing and phone use, thereby making a customer service into a pain-point, why not do a much better job of directing customers to lower-cost self-help online for those basic questions and focus our efforts on more complex technical problems?

> **It is critical to approach the process of turning our legacy investments (including our stores) into strengths with self-awareness and to avoid the sunk-cost trap of defending what we have simply because we have it.**

Our customers are a powerful help in that process. If we listen to them, they will tell us what matters and what doesn't.

Some lessons from the best in class

There's a huge danger in trying to boil down everything that has happened to retailers over the last couple of decades into a small number of big ideas. Reality is always more complex than that. But if there is a single thing that could be said to differentiate retailers that have thrived from those that have suffered over this period, it is this challenge of being clear about the role of the store and then executing on it.

A consequence of the 'Old Normal' world of high transaction costs was that retail stores were very often there because they were the only way of buying something. Critical success factors in that world were having the right products in the right place at the right time, merchandising them clearly and having an efficiently run set of store processes.

In some sectors, additional factors also came into play. Luxury products needed to be displayed in an environment that showed them in a premium way, but too many retail businesses became too focused on operational processes and expanding the sheer number of stores, without giving enough focus to what might happen when customers faced a choice of other places to buy.

That's not to diminish the skill involved in running a retail store in the pre-New Normal world. Simply getting the right products into store, well displayed and with a well-trained staff on hand is a huge feat. Good retailing distinguished itself from bad retailing in a way we'd still recognise today – products cleverly displayed not only to encourage purchases but also to encourage adding just one more thing into your basket, clean and well-looked-after stores that people wanted to come into, and staff who were proud to work for the brand.

But in the New Normal, if we really listen to why customers might come into a store, the answers have changed. No longer is the store the only place to buy or browse. Indeed, for many product categories it is by far the least convenient channel in which to do either of those things. In the New Normal, the purpose of the store is not just to get the product into the customers' hands.

Instead, it is to encourage the discovery of products, to educate customers on their use and to get customers to want to join the brand, sometimes metaphorically but sometimes literally in the case of businesses with membership or subscription products. For those sweets in the service station, sometimes the shop remains the only port of call (and we can price accordingly), but those are rare situations which have become the exception rather than the rule.

Consider these emerging retail titans:

- In **Lush,** the cosmetic business, stores are about demonstrating product in the most visual way possible. Stores are filled with sinks so that team members and customers can unwrap bars and open pots and really try products. One of the hallmarks of 'old retail' was a focus on stock shrinkage – measuring precisely how much stock failed to turn into sales because it was wasted, stolen or otherwise used up in the sales process. The Lush business turns that on its head by positively encouraging the use of product, recognising that the chatty, immersive and (literally) bubbly experience that you have during a product demo will make you a customer for life and more than pay back.

- In **Games Workshop,** an extraordinary chain of shops selling war-gaming action figures, the staff and customers are always either playing a game on a table-top battlefield or painting some new figures. A million miles from simply having rows of products in boxes, this is a store where interaction is everything and deliberately so. Every child (or adult) recruited into the hobby will spend hours and hundreds of pounds on their hobby, so every tutorial, game and introductory talk for new players is worth its weight in gold.

- In **Apple** stores every product is available to play with and every member of staff is a well-trained brand advocate ready to help you there and then. No mobile brand before Apple would have dared to design stores like that – terrified as they were of expensive devices being shoplifted. Apple stores are massively profitable in their own right, but their role as brand 'recruitment centres' vastly outweighs their direct revenue importance or any cost of lost stock.

- In **Timpsons,** a UK chain of shoe repair and dry-cleaning shops, the social causes important to the business come to the fore and great autonomy is given to the local teams to bring that to life. A famous example is the offer to clean an outfit for anyone unemployed and looking for work for free to help them get work.

- **Hotel Chocolat** has enthusiastic staff offering tasting samples like confectionery drug dealers and both displays and packages its products like the aspirational, high-end gifts you want to buy. Even selling a product which is broadly comparable to those available in supermarkets or elsewhere, it has used its physical retail stores to create and maintain a strongly differentiated brand and a resultant price premium.

Some lessons from those which didn't make it

But for every one of these inspiring examples are a long list of other brands which have not really grasped what their stores are for. Consider the toy industry and the famous, depressing example of Toys R Us. Once the giant of the toy industry and the first port of call for parents looking for birthday and Christmas presents, the business gradually faded and lost market share before finally, and tragically, going into administration.

Much has been written about why that happened. Online competition is often cited as a factor. So is the gradual shift of retailing from 'big box' shops to smaller outlets. Private equity ownership and associated indebtedness have come under the microscope too.

> **There's at least a grain of truth in all these post-mortem verdicts, but there is another and more important factor that explains the decline of Toys R Us and that is just how dull its stores were.**

It seems extraordinary that you could take a 40,000 square foot store, fill it with every toy under the sun and end up with a painfully dull retail experience. But somehow the business managed it. Years of cost-cutting and reducing staff numbers took all advice and interactivity out of the store, leaving miles of shelves of dusty boxes in their place.

Once you do that, any and all of the other factors listed above will kill your business. If I can shop elsewhere, compare prices easily and avoid visiting your dusty cavern then I will. And Toys R Us customers did exactly that.

Imagine if the interactivity and joie de vivre of a Lush or a Games Workshop (the latter operating out of stores a fiftieth the size of Toys R Us) was applied to a massive toy emporium. Colleagues on every aisle, opening toys and organising demonstrations. Nerf ball fights around the store. Talks and coffee for parents of tiny ones with all the latest educational toys lying around to see which ones got drooled over most.

It should have been possible to make Toys R Us stores into every parent and child's favourite weekend destination, and in doing so to maintain market share in a strong sector and keep the business going. But it would have taken investment rather than staff reductions. It would have taken brave financial leadership, sacrificing short-term profit for long-term viability. It would have taken new and innovative commercial models – toy of the month subscriptions? It would have taken early and effective investment in online channels to complement the store and deliver the brand experience a little bit to the home.

> **It would have taken a clear vision of what stores (and toy stores in particular) are actually for in the New Normal.**

What role can they play in building relationships with customers that make them want to come back again and again? The answer to that question has changed in the last 20 years – and a business which didn't change with it could not keep up.

Bringing it together

The challenge of location strategy in the New Normal is this fundamental. It's not just about how many stores, or which towns to put them in. It is about finding a purpose for physical and people-driven relationships with your customers and creating places that bring that to life.

Walk down your high street and look into the stores there. Ask yourself how many of them are really bringing their brands to life in the way we've shown here and how many, on the other hand, are just laying out product and hoping people turn up.

Getting stores right is mission-critical for retailers facing new competition in the New Normal. And one outcome from it is all too common. The realisation that our historical expertise and ability to advise and support our customers is an asset, not just because it recruits more customers but because it supports another critical economic goal: turning a single transaction into a long-term customer relationship. We'll explore the transformative power of customer relationships in the next rule.

Chapter

5

Rule 5: Knowing your customer is key – flying blind won't end well

You meet someone at a party. They make a good impression, they seem interesting and interested in you. A connection is made.

Then it all unravels. You meet them again, in a different place under different circumstances. Oddly, they've forgotten who you are altogether and when you remind them the conversation takes a really weird turn. They appear to be an entirely different person and reveal a totally different set of interests and values. Far from being interested in you, they make it clear that they couldn't care less and are much more interested in someone else they've just met.

Unsettling, isn't it? There's a good reason for that. There are a whole raft of psychological disorders which have this appearance of rapidly changing personality as one of their symptoms. We are programmed at a very deep level to find this kind of thing unpleasant and to run a mile from it. And yet, as brands we do this to our customers all the time.

Two cardinal sins

There are two cardinal sins we can commit each time we interact with a current or potential customer.

The first is to be careless about how we present ourselves.

> **A consumer's view of our brand is simply the sum of all the interactions they have with our business.**

That includes the carefully designed marketing material that a team has sweated over and checked for brand consistency, but it also includes casual conversations with our employees in a store, the impression given by home delivery drivers (even when they don't work for our business but are sub-contractors) and the experience of calling into one of our call centres.

If those interactions are wildly inconsistent with each other, and also change over time, we are giving exactly the off-putting impression to our customers that the weird party guest does. Marketing material which is designed to give a brand impression of quality and high-end design can be rendered pointless by carelessly designed packaging or a 'pile em high' retail experience. All our efforts to present our brand as one which really values each and every customer can be undermined by a careless or uninterested colleague who talks to our customers and represents that same brand.

> **Indeed, the opposite is also true. Every day retail professionals are doing a terrific job to delight customers on behalf of brands which then let unfriendly policies or shoddy products undo all that hard work.**

Consider again the incredible story of Apple. Obviously, at the core of its success has been the creation of amazing products like the iPhone and the iPad, but behind those products sits a deeper story. Spend any time in the headquarters in Cupertino or talk to people who knew and worked with Steve Jobs during this period of the revival of the brand, and the thing you'll hear more than anything else is the story of an obsessive focus on what the Apple brand should mean, what it should stand for and how that should be presented in an absolutely consistent way throughout every part of the customer journey.

The story of Jobs obsessively and painstakingly choosing the colours for iMacs is well known, but when you put that product focus together with the same laser-like attention to detail being applied to packaging, to the design and staffing of Apple stores and to every other area where the business connected with its customers, you begin to see why the brand became the dominant world-beater that it did.

You can like or loathe the Apple eco-system of products, but you can't deny that it delivers an absolutely clear and consistent brand experience, something very few other businesses can really say they achieve.

Action planning

How consistently delivered is your brand experience?

One danger for retailers is that it is almost impossible for leaders in the business to experience the brand the same way customers do. Inevitably, when you walk into a store it is for a visit and, even if you pop in over the weekend to buy something, you'll be recognised.

Beyond the store experience are other dangers, though. Do you receive the same marketing materials that your customers do, and if so, do you read it the way they would? If you have one of your own loyalty cards, did you have to fill in the application form or did someone in marketing just bring you one? If you need to talk to the call centre, do you ring the same number and wait in the same queue as your customers or do you just walk over and talk to the team leader directly?

It's a good idea to get as close as possible to experiencing your brand the way your customers do. Even to the extent that you can't, it can be a powerful exercise to populate the wall of a meeting room with all the material you expect customers to read – not just the carefully crafted marketing but the deliver slips, returns notes and till receipts – and see if they paint the picture of your brand that you'd hope they would.

As if it isn't bad enough that we do an inconsistent job of presenting ourselves to our customers, the second cardinal sin makes that even worse. If we fail to recognise or remember a customer when we interact with them, we also can't possibly be building a lasting or valuable relationship with them. If I forget your name every time

I see you, and you have to re-introduce yourself to me, I won't be doing a great job of earning your trust or encouraging you to give me your money.

Know your customer – and their shirts

In my line of work, I'm often asked about my favourite experiences as a customer. For many years, I'd often say that my favourite customer experience was the one delivered by the dry-cleaner at the end of my road. (I'd still say that, but I've long since moved house, and my shirts have never been the same.)

The dry-cleaning service was very good, with all the little touches that you get from a small family-owned business rather than an outlet of a big national chain. But what really made the experience of being its customer stand out was that they knew who I was. Not only did that mean something socially (they'd ask about my kids, we'd complain about the local traffic and all the usual things), but it also meant that they were able to treat me like an individual. If I needed a rush job, that was fine. Once, they handed me back a dress shirt and pointed out that they'd replaced a button that I hadn't even noticed was missing, because they knew that cleaning a dress shirt probably meant I had an event to go to that evening (which was true).

This is the stock in trade of small businesses the world over. Knowing your customers, treating the regular ones as special and valued, as if they and you were members of the human race rather than just faceless representatives of a 'brand ethos'.

Really good small businesses make a virtue of their smallness and their localness by knowing their customers, being a part of their local community and as a result make themselves easier, more fun and more rewarding to do business with.

Big businesses with bad memories

One of the costs of growth as our businesses get bigger is that we inevitably get more distant from our customers. Not only do the owners and operators of the business end up in a head office some-where rather than standing behind a till and talking to people, but inevitably customers cease to be individuals and become just a statistic.

I once asked a big retailer who its most valuable customer was. It had an answer, but it involved graphs and pie charts. "Our most valuable customer is typically in this kind of demographic, visits us this many times a year and buys these kinds of products when she does so." You know the kind of thing. Most businesses could do the same – answer my question in terms of segments, demograph-ics and statistics.

That wasn't what I meant though. I wanted the actual name of the most valuable customer. When I said so, the big retailer looked at me like I was mad. But the point was made. A small local business will have at least an intuitive ability to recognise its most regular and most valuable customers. They will come out from behind the counter and say hello, and make sure that they go the extra mile to earn and retain the loyalty of that customer. Almost inevitably, though, a larger business loses the ability to do that.

For some, it is easier. If your business is based on subscription, membership or some other regular payment, you will at least end up with a database of customers, and by interrogating that database you can find your most valuable customer relationships. Gyms, mobile phone networks, broadband and utility companies all enjoy this advantage. You might not know each customer personally, but it is at least possible to make sure that your teams are focused on keeping them happy. You can also work out what percentage of your overall business comes from those most loyal customers, and the results can be striking.

> **I worked with a business where 10% of the customer base accounted for over 40% of the revenue. Well worth keeping those customers happy!**

For retailers, however, such a database of customers is harder to come by. If your business model is based on occasional purchases or purchases by customers who don't have to identify themselves, then it can be much harder to sort out who is who.

Just listen to the language of most retail businesses when they talk about their quarterly results. The maths of a subscription-based business is quite simple. How many customers do you have and how much do they spend on average? Multiply those two numbers together and you have your revenue. It even looks a bit like the formula for customer lifetime value (CLV) we encountered earlier.

For a retailer, however, those two numbers are very hard to calculate. Without a customer database they will stop talking about how many customers they have and start talking instead about footfall, the number of people who walked into their store, a figure which takes no account of whether the same customers come back multiple times or not. Similarly, instead of talking about spend per customer they will talk about average basket size or average purchase. Again, a number which takes no account of who is doing the buying.

Footfall multiplied by sales conversion and average basket size will also give a retailer their revenue figure, but these metrics are so much less meaningful than number of customers and spend per customer. They tell us nothing about who is coming more often, nothing about loyalty and they don't allow us to calculate how much of our business is coming from our most valuable customers. As such, they are anonymous and encourage us to consider all customers as the same, which is tantamount to considering all customers as interchangeable and replaceable. Something which would have horrified my dry cleaner.

The loyalty card paradox

The value of becoming a business that really knows which customers are spending what is demonstrated by the huge efforts that retailers have gone to over the last few decades to build loyalty programmes. World-famous examples like the Tesco Clubcard and the multi-brand Nectar programme have been joined by dozens of other schemes from retailers, restaurants, service stations and many other businesses.

The description 'loyalty programme' is a misnomer. Although on the face of it these schemes are designed to offer incentives to shop more often or to spend a little bit more, the evidence for how much they really change consumer behaviour is patchy at best.

Consumer response to incentives is fairly straightforward. If you offer me a discount on something I was going to buy anyway, I will certainly use it but that isn't really changing my behaviour. It's just giving me money. If, on the other hand, you offer me a discount on something I wasn't thinking of buying, or on a much larger purchase size than I was thinking of making, then I will think about it a bit more carefully, and I will certainly put a lower value on your 'reward', recognising that you are trying to reward yourself as much as you are reward me.

As a result, loyalty programmes end up being a juggling match for brands. Torn between offering rewards that customers like and use (which therefore make the scheme attractive but also make it expensive) or offering tricky and gimmicky rewards that seem to cost less but in fact also leave customers cold. Some brands get this balancing act more right than others, but the fact still remains that generating an actual and measurable increase in revenues on a particular product line is often tricky and expensive to achieve through loyalty card promotions.

Indeed, if you are going to offer a reward for customers spending more, more often, then usually the most effective loyalty scheme is the tried and tested stamp card. These have a number of empty slots and simply require the cashier to use a stamp every time a customer makes a purchase. Once the card is full, a free purchase or some other reward is delivered. These cards have downsides in that they are easy to defraud, but they involve almost no IT expenditure, don't need rooms full of expensive marketers and deliver a straightforward benefit to customers that they value.

Many old-time retailers have used the mixed evidence of sales uplifts from loyalty programmes to opt out of them altogether. They tell themselves, and their stock-holders, that sales promotions (including the stamp cards) simply work better than loyalty programmes in generating additional sales, and that more complex schemes are just that – nerdy, technology-hungry projects that commercial marketers like because they win awards, but which are not the best return on investment for the proper retail business.

> **This argument completely misses the point. The reason 'loyalty programme' is a misnomer is because the real value in these schemes is not in generating behaviour, but in measuring it.**

By getting to a point where at least some of the transactions being done through the till every day can be tied back to specific customers, whose overall behaviour can therefore be modelled and tracked, a business buys itself the most precious commodity it can have: a view of what is really happening across the customer base, and an actionable view of who those customers really are.

Suddenly a retail business which saw lots of transactions, but could rarely identify one customer from another, begins to look more like a subscription business, which can track the different needs, behaviours and purchases of each individual customer.

The power of customer data

And why is that important? Let's think about some of the things you can do when you can see individual customer transactions:

- Obviously, by identifying your most valuable customers, you can take action to protect and grow their relationship with your brand. You might indeed offer them discounts, but you might also ensure they get a first look at your new stock or early access to hot new products. Even actions as simple as acknowledging their loyalty and asking their opinion about aspects of your business can make sure that you move from having one-way, broadcast-marketing exchanges with your customers to having those genuine, two-way, relationship-building conversations.

- Knowing who your customers are also creates an opportunity for timely crisis management. If a valuable customer suddenly stops buying from you, it is worth figuring out why. The subscription businesses we talked about know that investing in avoiding or recovering 'churn' (customers who end their subscription) is worth at least as much as acquiring new customers, and indeed most such businesses will spend more on retention activities than they do on acquisition. Viewed from that perspective it is extraordinary to think that most retailers have no ability to engage in that activity. They literally can't see when a high-value customer stops turning up, with the result that more than half of the marketing efforts that a subscription business might engage in are lost to them.

- Knowing who your valuable customers are also guides investment and product decisions in the longer term too. You might create a special premium product designed around the needs of those customers. Some of the most successful cinema businesses in the world have invested heavily in premium offers with inclusive food and drink and terrific reserved seating – offerings designed precisely to appeal to their most regular and most valuable customers. Indeed, some consumer businesses have taken their emulation of subscription offerings to its literal conclusion, creating a tier of service where paying a fixed amount each month gets you a regular delivery of product. This creates convenience and simplicity for the customer but also harnesses the incredible power of regular data for the brand. That doesn't have to be the preserve of high-end or expensive products, either, as Dollar Shave Club demonstrates so clearly.

More generally, having reliable data on individual customer behaviours unlocks a wide range of potential actions a business can take. The modern science of 'machine learning' is all about using sophisticated computer models to work out not only what to do with your most valuable customers but also how to increase the value of every customer relationship. So, working out the next product to recommend or the best action the business can take to encourage everyone to buy just a little more often.

Machine learning models are powerful but they require one key fuel: data about past customer behaviour (at an individual level) with which to build models that can predict likely future behaviour.

So, knowing your customer well has huge value for retailers. Not only does it allow them to emulate the service and customer relationship skills of my dry cleaner, but it also unlocks the opportunity to invest in retaining, growing and learning from the set of customers who generate the greatest revenue and profit.

> If it is true for a subscription business like the one I worked for that 10% of the customers generated 40% of the revenue, then that is almost certainly true for most retail brands today too. The only difference is that most of them don't know which 10% of their customers it is that matter so much.

In a business world where so much is changing, flying blind by not knowing your customers is incredibly dangerous. Indeed, the growth of online and mobile channels creates opportunities for generating customer data (since by definition you know the identity of someone who has purchased online with a credit card), but also highlights the need to carry that customer knowledge across channel. Imagine your most valuable online customer walking into one of your stores and not being recognised and treated appropriately. Something that happens for most brands every day.

And so, although it has always been important to know your customer, here is our next rule of the New Normal: **knowing your customer is more important now than it has ever been.**

Data, insight and hard cash

I once worked with an online business with an interesting problem. It believed in the service it was providing and had a way to generate revenue from the traffic it got from customers, both through advertising and from businesses to whom it was connecting those customers.

The problem was that it couldn't make the sums add up.

As they articulated it, the marketing and other costs associated with attracting a new consumer on to their site were higher than the revenues they could generate from that transaction. Crudely, it was costing them £1 to get the visit and they were making 70p in revenue as a result.

Now some internet businesses have been able to ignore that maths, getting larger and larger while generating more and more losses in the hope that scale or some divine intervention would eventually turn traffic into profit. But those businesses are usually based in Silicon Valley.

The online business I was talking to was based in London and had investors who were a bit less tolerant of burgeoning losses and were quite enthusiastic to understand what the path to profit looked like.

As far as the management team was concerned, the strategic review process had looked at both sides of the problem. If £1 of acquisition cost generated only 70p of income, then the task was either to reduce the acquisition cost per customer or increase the revenue on each transaction. There were indeed some opportunities to do both of those things, by optimising the searchability of the site and by improving its layout so that fewer visitors left without transacting. It seemed, however, too difficult to close the whole gap between acquisition cost and revenue and the board was worried.

It took us an embarrassingly long time to work out that there is another solution to this maths problem. Rather than making the £1 per new customer go down, or the 70p per transaction go up, why not just get more transactions from each new customer? If each £1 investment in attracting someone to the site results in a stream of 70p transactions rather than just one, the economics of the business is transformed totally. The right strategy for the business was one which was designed to create that stream. That's partly about the basics, of course. Making sure that the transaction was easy enough and useful enough for the consumer that they wanted to come back.

It is also about ensuring that the business is deliberately engineered to creating lasting customer relationships rather than isolated transactions. That might mean having customers sign in so that

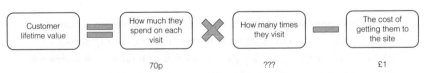

Figure 5.1 Customer lifetime value for online businesses

the business can remind them later at some appropriate time to come back. It might mean building in incentives to transact more than once (a bonus benefit on the third transaction, for example). One way or another, creating the relationship and the reason to come back again was mission-critical for that business.

I use the example of a web business because the maths is particularly easy. Usually in such a business it is fairly straightforward to calculate the cost of acquiring a 'visit' because it is made up from the costs of advertising on other websites or buying results places in search engines. It is also often easy to calculate the return on an individual customer visit, particularly if, like my example, the business is providing a referral service to other brands and makes its revenue from referral fees which are fairly transparent.

In a bigger and more complex business, the equation of revenue from transactions less the cost of generating those transactions can be harder to isolate in such a purist way. A restaurant chain gets its visitors through a whole variety of marketing means including responses to coupons and adverts but also people simply wandering in attracted by the signage and the menu board outside. Not so easy to generate a 'cost per visit' in such a multi-channel environment. On the other hand, it is fairly easy for that restaurant to work out the revenue and profit for each transaction from analysing the bills given to each table.

For other types of hospitality businesses (and many others), the situation can be even less clear. Not only does a shopping centre have the same issues calculating cost per visit, but it can also be hard to isolate the income from that visit when it is often split across several transactions (at the food court, in different shops).

No matter the difficulties in calculating the same equation as our web business example, however, the underlying logic remains the same.

> **It costs money to acquire customers and generate interest in your business. If you can turn that interest into repeated purchases rather than just single isolated purchases, it will make a huge difference to the profitability of your business.**

Customer lifetime value (CLV) revisited

We've come across the analytical term for this already in our discussion of Rule 2: customer lifetime value. The longer you keep a customer and the more repeat visits you generate, the higher their value to you. The cost of acquiring a customer can vary enormously from business to business, from a few pence for a website to hundreds of pounds for a mobile company. In either case, the important thing is ensuring that the value returned from that customer is higher than the cost, and the easiest way to do that is to ensure that they stay a customer as long as possible.

The language and toolset of CLV is very familiar for subscription businesses, and increasingly for online businesses, precisely because it is fairly easy to measure. It is fascinating by comparison to consider that many retailer, branded consumer goods companies and hospitality businesses not only don't maximise CLV, but they don't even know what it is to start with.

In our discussion of Rule 2 we talked about CLV as a way to articulate the value of doing the right thing by customers in the short term, if that is an important driver to keeping them for the longer term. The long-term reward from a satisfied customer can be much greater than the short-term benefit of the hidden charge or cancellation fee that they pay, but makes them swear never to come back.

Now we can generalise from that to see that there are a wide range of tools we can deploy if our goal is to maximise the value of every customer we have. From product ranges designed for different types of customer right through to sophisticated computer models helping us to sell them more, there is a lot we can do if only we have the data to do so.

Maximising the lifetime value of your relationship with a customer starts with knowing who they are – not at a theoretical level based on segmentation and customer stereotypes but at an individual level. What do they buy and how often? What is important to them about your product? Is it the specification, the after-sales service or the perceived value your brand delivers? Could they buy from one of your competitors or do they already?

That's all fairly easy to find out if you are a subscription business, or one which in some other way has an ongoing billing relationship with your customers.

Retail and the data challenge

It is much harder to build your business around CLV if you are a multi-channel retailer with a small flow of customer data and therefore less ability to build models of future behaviour at an individual customer level. However, there are things that we can do to ensure that our customer databases are as rich as possible:

- Give customers a reason to identify themselves when they buy from you. This is the real value of the retailer loyalty scheme which exists not so much to create additional purchases but rather to act as an information-gathering mechanic where none might otherwise exist. Loyalty schemes can range from the sophisticated points-based 'earn and burn' loyalty programmes through to simple stamp card-based mechanics or even to simply asking for, and recording, an email address at the till. What links all these ideas together is that when they are done well, they are generating identifiable customer data. Even the 'Get eight stamps and get a free coffee' cards can achieve this, but not if they are simple dumb bits of paper. Some kind of barcode linked to the till can ensure that the valuable data gets where it needs to.

- Encourage this data-gathering across your channels. If you sell both online and through retail stores, you are already building up a rich set of data from your online customers. By definition, you can see what they've ordered, but with careful management you can also see what they've looked at and clicked on but not yet purchased – valuable profiling data. You can even generate this kind of profiling data deliberately by suggesting products to customers and then analysing their responses. Rich data from online customers is incomplete, however, without the additional visibility of purchases through your retail channel, and indeed the partial picture given by online-only data can be very misleading. How can you encourage those online customers to identify themselves when they buy through one of your stores? What incentive can you give them to want to link their store purchases to their online account?

- Find other ways to use technology to build models of CLV. One simple example is to offer free WiFi in your stores or service centres. Properly set up, a WiFi service will ask the customer to use their email address to register and log in. As soon as they do, you develop the ability to link those store visits with online purchases, and to see how often individual customers visit (or even walk past) which of your stores. This kind of technology is a formidable and often overlooked data source. One business I worked with added a million new contactable customers to their 4 million database within a single quarter of changing their WiFi offering in this way.

There are complex choices to be made in each of these areas, and a range of technology options from the 'quick and dirty' to the much more sophisticated. But the prize is worth it.

Bringing it together

Consider this scenario. As a multi-channel business, you've always had a database of customers and some reasonable analysis of what they buy from you. However, by investing in better web analytics capability you now also have rich data about the products those customers have looked at online but not purchased. Because you have a simple loyalty programme offering rewards for each purchase, you've given your customers the desire to offer their online account details at the till when they buy in your store, and you've allowed them to use their touch-and-go payment cards to make that easy.

The WiFi in your stores is also an attractive service and adds further to your data by showing you which customers visit the physical store but don't buy anything. With careful use of geo-tagging technology you can even see which departments those customers visit and what path they take through the store, and because that is linked back to the wider customer database you can do that analysis both for high-value customers as well as lower-value ones to understand any differences.

With all this data at hand, you have invested in customer analytics capability and data scientists, and they are building models for you of the CLV of different customers and also aggregating that information up so you can understand individual store catchment areas and broad customer segments. As a result, you are actively marketing to any high-value customers who stop buying from you, and are also building models predicting the kinds of products each customer might be interested in buying next so that your marketing campaigns stop being broad shouting exercises and become tailored and bespoke to each customer.

Sounds fantastic, doesn't it? And also a long way from the current position of most retailers. And yet the individual steps necessary to get to that place are not huge, and require only well-proven technology. The exercise of working out how to get there will not only require technology, but a careful review of commercial policies, pricing and marketing, particularly if you are to create an incentive for customers to identify themselves to you which works for them but doesn't break the bank for you.

And remember the prize. Multiplying the number of sales made from each newly acquired customer is hugely profitable. There is also a knock-on impact on the battle with your competitors, both existing and new.

> **The business which can turn a new customer into the highest CLV can also, by extension, afford to invest the most in acquiring them in the first place.**

In the long run, the business with the highest CLV will grow market share by simply out-gunning everyone else. Best make sure that is you.

As we've talked about the link between online and physical sales channels, we've begun to demonstrate the inverse of the Sun Tzu quote from earlier. As important as it is to know yourself, it is also important to understand your competitors and the new world of technology from which they are emerging. As much therefore as we need to reinvent our businesses for the New Normal, we also need to reinvent ourselves as business leaders. We'll talk more about that in Part 2.

But first, let's move on to the next rule of the New Normal as we explore the strange pic-n-mix world of dis-intermediation.

Chapter

Rule 6: If a product or process can be dis-intermediated or simplified, it will be

As we discovered with our New Normal rule about location, transaction costs matter a lot. When they are high, we tend not to shop around all that much and don't look for too many competitive quotes. So the way that businesses distribute their products, ensuring that we trip over them often, is a big driver of profitability.

It is arguable, in fact, that one of the biggest changes that the internet, social media and the always-on mobile economy have created is that they have effectively reduced the difficulty, and therefore the time and money cost of doing things. We can gather information at a click of a button, can shop without leaving the house and can even check a store's price on a key product from inside the shop of a competitor. All of that has made it easier for consumers to get a great deal and have consequently changed the rules for business.

But there is another, and equally far-reaching, way in which lower transaction costs have made it hard for some traditional businesses but have also created opportunities where none existed before. That is in allowing consumers to 'unbundle' or disconnect different parts of a service from each other, and shop around separately for each part.

The lesson from your holiday

Consider holidays and leisure travel. Once upon a time, we went to the travel agent, gave them a rough idea of where we wanted to go and how much we had to spend and the outcome was usually a package tour of one kind or other. We'd pay a holiday company (through the travel agent, who in turn was taking a commission) and that company would provide us with the flight, the transfers at the far end, the hotel accommodation and usually a set of excursions or optional extras and some or all of the meals for our holiday.

What a service like that offered in a world where information-gathering was difficult and transaction costs were high was much-needed convenience. We didn't need to research lots of different parts of our holiday or trudge from shop to shop buying them. We had no real ability to compare the services of one hotel with another and so it was both easier and cheaper to entrust the creation of our overall holiday to a single company and its high-street representatives.

As we've seen already, the holiday market has changed beyond recognition now. We can review hotels and restaurants by reading the opinions of thousands of our fellow travellers. We can compare flight prices online at the click of a button. We can find excursions and experiences on the other side of the world and decide whether they are for us. It has never been easier for us to construct our own holidays piece by piece, making a personal choice about each element and ending up with an overall experience tailored for our budgets, interests and families.

In the language of the economist, the holiday company has been dis-intermediated. Consumers can bypass them and go and buy the constituent parts of their holiday directly from the suppliers – roughly akin to being able to buy your vegetables directly from the farmer just the same way your supermarket does.

By the way, none of this should be taken to mean that there isn't still value in buying a package holiday from an experienced holiday company. Although smaller than it once was, the package holiday segment remains an active and profitable one, and indeed in some parts of the market there are even signs that holiday companies are growing their share of customers' wallets.

What has changed totally, however, is the reason consumers buy from these companies. Where once it was about convenience and the lack of an effective alternative, we are now in a world where most aspects of a package deal could indeed be recreated by a traveller willing to put in a bit of effort. So why doesn't everyone do it for themselves?

One clue is in the word 'effort'. There is no doubt that one under-pinning feature of the holiday package market today remains that they make it easy for their guests. Another key word, however, is 'trust'. If a holiday company can reliably build a brand which indicates to consumers that it will come up with options for their holiday which are safe, simple and deliver a great experience then it will still win business.

What was once an excuse to earn margin from some parts of an experience to cross-subsidise others is now instead a consumer service. Indeed, the very best holiday companies now look more like concierge services: constructing packages based on their exper-tise and experience and selling them to consumers on exactly that basis. Price still matters too, of course. Another reason holiday companies are still in business is that buying thousands of hotel rooms ought to offer some scale economics when compared to a traveller buying one or two.

Unbundling is everywhere

This dis-intermediation is all around us, enabled by the free and easy exchange of information online. Here are some examples:

- Taxi companies have been cut out of the loop by platforms like Uber, which allow us to effectively charge each other for offer-ing lifts.

- Hotels, fresh from dis-intermediating the holiday companies by doing business with us directly, have had the same thing done to them by AirBnB allowing us to rent rooms directly to each other.

- Banks used to build their consumer businesses around the idea that if they could get us to take a basic current account with them, we would by default also do our savings, take our mortgage and borrow to buy our car from them. As financial services have moved online and become easier to purchase, that has changed entirely to the point where the traditional (and loss-making) current account product is a real problem for many banks.

- Even in the retail sector bundles are being 'un-bundled'. Many electronics retailers used to keep themselves afloat despite the incredibly low margins that they can get on laptops and TVs by adding in extended warranties and other services that themselves had a much higher margin. Now that we can easily find out online what a warranty company will charge us directly to insure our products, that opportunity is much diminished.

- Another kind of un-bundling which impacts many retailers is the fact that it is getting harder and harder to position high-margin products (accessories, bolt-ons) next to low-margin core products and use bundle-selling to make the economics work. Higher-margin products attract disproportionate competition, particularly from online specialists, leaving the high-street retailer in danger of selling only low-margin items that render the store unprofitable. In a New Normal where it is perfectly easy to cross-check prices on products from inside a retailer's own store (sometimes using their own WiFi), margin opportunities get harder to find.

Here, then, is our final rule of the New Normal. If it can be dis-intermediated, then it probably will be.

Three reasons why we still buy bundles

Just as with the holiday example, instances of customers bypassing traditional suppliers, or splitting what used to be a single purchase into different components bought separately, do not mean that historical businesses don't exist anymore. People still take cabs despite the existence of Uber.

What it does mean though is that those businesses should think very carefully about why customers would buy a bundled or aggregated service from them if they could put the components together themselves. One answer to that might be that an older, less technologically savvy or more cautious audience segment still prefers to buy from the brand it trusts and is prepared to pay an effective premium for doing so. That's a comforting answer, but a risky one.

Very few industries survive for long once part of their market begins to purchase a different way by just relying on customers who haven't got around to changing yet.

Another answer, as with the holiday companies, is that some customers choose to appreciate the expertise, advice and support of a trusted intermediary. This role as advisor and guide is a really interesting one for some retailers to consider for themselves. If your competition is a massive online retailer willing to sell everything at cost (looking at you, Amazon), then one route forward is to head in the other direction. Instead of selling everything, try to sell the best of everything in your sector and wrap products together with advice and support that key customer segments actually value.

This is one of the reasons that in some sectors specialist retailers (online and off) continue to survive. Camping equipment, sports goods and cycling supplies all spring to mind. Later in this book, we will explore some techniques for doing exactly that. After all, no one criticises Hotel Chocolat for not selling every brand of chocolate.

A third reason why customers might continue to buy a package of goods or services in the face of dis-intermediation is economic. In some markets where purchasing power really matters and where retailers are effectively 'bulk breaking' by buying very large quantities of products and then selling them on in smaller, retail quantities (like food retail), these scale economics make a big difference to the structure of the industry, institutionalising the power of large, strong retailers. Your idea to dis-intermediate the supermarkets with a 'vegetables on demand' service will always struggle against the realities of buying power.

Action planning

What is your un-bundling risk? Does a disproportionate amount of your profit come from one product or product category?

If so, could a new competitor spring up that only sold that product, putting you in a position where you only have the lower margin sales left?

Alternatively, is your higher-margin product line vulnerable to substitution of a different kind – for example, from an alternative technology in the way that DVDs have faced competition from online streaming?

Two contradictory strategies – and why they are both right

For those of us in consumer businesses, there are two useful things to reflect on about dis-intermediation.

The first is how we might continue to be able to sell our bundles. Which of the answers we've just discussed might keep our customers coming to us? That is a powerful topic because really embracing why customers should buy our aggregated products and services will mean making sure that we really deliver on the benefit we are offering.

There are several kinds of bundling we can do to reduce the danger of being cherry-picked by competitors:

- The obvious and traditional retail answer is in **merchandising.** By displaying products together that go well together we can not only encourage people to buy them together but even create demand by increasing awareness of a product that customers didn't know they needed. Whether that is clothing accessories beautifully displayed with core dresses and suits, or fast-charging devices displayed with power-hungry mobile phones, encouraging up- and cross-sales through merchandising is a retail staple.

- Beyond simply displaying products together, we can **price them together** too. By offering discounts when products are bought together, we can make the linkage even stronger and also reduce the ability for online cherry-pickers to make a simple price comparison. Creating a single price for a bundle of products is stronger still. There is a reason that games consoles (very low margin) are usually sold bundled with three or four games. A bundle like that not only blunts the force of price comparison, but it can also hugely increase the margin generated from the sale.

- Less conventional, but just as powerful, is **creating bundles over time.** If a customer is going to regularly purchase a product (pet food, oil for the car, household cleaning products, you name it) and we create the ability to simply place a regular order, then we again protect ourselves from cherry-picking, lock in additional revenue from occasions where the customer might have bought from a competitor and also generate a recurring revenue stream. All great for customer lifetime value as we have seen earlier.

- The ultimate bundle, in some senses, is the **subscription.** Taking recurring purchase to its logical conclusion, if we can offer customers an 'all you can eat' service where they have access to a range of products whenever they want it because they are a member of our club or subscriber to our service, then we unlock all sorts of benefits. The revenue from a subscription is recurring and reliable, the 'all you can eat' offering tends to attract and then lock in our highest value customers and we get all the data and analytics benefits that we've already discussed elsewhere.

This is an enticing list, but there is an important caveat. None of these strategies is easy, and customers will see through a cobbled-together bundle instantly.

> **If you believe that you offer an expert, guided and valuable service to customers, or a carefully curated and high-quality range of products that people will be prepared to pay a premium for, you'd better be right.**

At the exact same time as the holiday companies were first being squeezed by customers choosing to design their own holidays, many of them also allowed the quality of the high-street travel agency experience to drop. In the face of a declining market, they were trying to control costs, but it was exactly the wrong thing to do. If you had any doubt about whether it would be cheaper and easier to build your own holiday, sitting in a travel agency while the agent used the same websites you could use from home and thumbed through a brochure without appearing to know any more about the holidays than you did, would soon remove any doubt.

A healthy fear of being bypassed or unbundled by competitors and by our own customers can become a galvanising call to action for a business. If the secret of our brand is expertise, then we need to work hard to bring that to life, with implications for recruitment, training and incentives all around our business. Equally, if our strength rests on scale economies and buying power then we'd better make that real too. Watching the massive supermarkets get hugely undercut on prices for groceries in the last decade by small new entrants who only have a fraction of their scale is a salutary reminder that economies of scale are hard work, not God-given.

We should not, however, use our analysis of why customers might continue to buy from us as an 'It will never happen to me' set of excuses. I once heard a very senior executive of a big telecoms company proudly explain that most of the value of the business came from complexity – from customers over-paying for services they didn't really understand. Needless to say, its share price hasn't performed very well since then, as customers have come to understand better and better where they are getting a valuable bundle of services and where, on the other hand, they are just getting ripped off.

The second possible dis-intermediation strategy, of course, is to do it ourselves. Just like the wider impact of the growth of low-price online competitors we covered earlier, too many big brands have missed the opportunities that the digital world has created for a smart, narrowly focused and highly targeted dis-intermediation play.

> **None of the big taxi companies invented Uber. None of the big hotel chains invented AirBnB, but they are here and making a massive difference in those sectors.**

If you are a retailer of pet supplies and you think there is a market for a branded and narrowly focused service offering regular deliveries of flea-control product to cat and dog owners, then you have two choices. One is to deliver a service like that through your stores and website as part of your wider business. The other is to create a stand-alone service on the web with its own branding, recruiting customers directly.

In practice, you can follow the integrated route, follow the stand-alone route or do both at the same time (with common fulfilment and procurement, the additional cost of a distinctly branded web portal is minimal). The right option will depend on a specific market and product type, but a simple guide is this: if a market for a narrowly focused offering in a high-margin part of your business looks like it might form, you should take the first move and offer it yourself. Either by creating a distinct offering but using your buying power and customer knowledge to prevent others from taking the market from you, or by creating a service more closely aligned to your core brand and using your brand recognition and marketing bandwidth to achieve the same thing. Either way, it isn't acceptable to watch margin taken from you by new market entrants creating services you could have done first.

Bringing it together

So, the paradox of dis-intermediation is that our strategic response should be to challenge ourselves in both directions. How can we deliver valuable bundles on the one hand (so that we don't get picked off by others cherry-picking single parts of our value chain), but on the other hand how can we also satisfy any emerging demand for unbundled services by doing it first?

> **The resolution to this paradox is that both of these routes can generate value from different customers at different times, and can co-exist within the same company.**

And so now we've seen all the rules of the New Normal. Each of them is a statement which would have been laughed at, or simply made no sense 20 years ago, but now is obvious enough that it is easy to find examples of the rule in action.

New entrants will smash your product or service up into component parts and cherry-pick the best ones. They will sell your products online at basically cost price. Customers will find your business in new ways, will talk about you and form your brand reputation for you while you aren't looking. They will demand a real, personal and human relationship with your brand and your historical investment in brand-building. Retail stores and product development are on a knife-edge between being your competitive advantage and being the millstone around your neck.

Despite that, all this change creates huge opportunities. Whole new markets have emerged in the last few decades; new entrants now dominate many markets and it has never been easier to have a meaningful conversation with millions of customers (and millions of potential customers) all at the same time.

What we need, however, is to re-tool our businesses to ensure that we take advantage of those opportunities. Much of what has historically seemed self-evident in our industries is no longer true. Most particularly, what it took to become a successful business, and therefore the skills that it took to become a successful business leader, have all changed. For large and older businesses in particular, this can be a big challenge. How to throw out what no longer works and reinvent the business in the face of layers of middle and senior management who only know the old way to succeed, and for whom that process of reinvention must seem scary and threatening.

Looking ahead to Part 2

Every time a great retail business disappears from our high street, people ask the same question: How did this happen? Faced with a barrage of 'after the fact' analysis, the cause of the brand's problems sometimes seems so self-evident that the real question becomes "How did the leadership of the business not see this coming?"

As we've analysed the rules of the New Normal, we've caught glimpses of the reason for this apparent failure to react several times. The reality is that changing a business is difficult at the best of times. Any business is a huge coalition of interests including shareholders, suppliers, staff and customers, and anyone who has tried to shift a strategy or reposition a business knows how difficult it can be to get that unwieldy set of interests to align and support the new plan.

But the shift to the New Normal has complicated that change process still further, because not only does it require us to explore new business lines and new revenue opportunities, it also forces us to consider how to kill off, cannibalise, move away from or otherwise lose some of our key historic assets.

Retailers challenged by the New Normal find that pricing practices which have worked for decades no longer deliver. They find that sources of margin they have relied on suddenly disappear. They find newly empowered customers with choices they didn't have before and the ability to shift suppliers at the click of a button. They find that an organisation built on finding, securing and then operating more and more new stores each year suddenly needs to shrink, re-think and re-design its whole strategy on physical retail outlets.

These are demanding things for shareholders to grapple with. It is a brave investor who supports the destruction of a historic profit stream on the basis that it might unlock new sources of growth and prevent attacks from new entrants to the market. But they are also demanding for the teams who work in our business. In many cases, the skills and expertise demanded by the strategies we need to put in place are not the ones our colleagues have grown up with. Conversely, expertise that senior leaders have developed over decades can suddenly be worth less than it used to be in the New Normal.

This all-encompassing set of challenges presented to our businesses by the New Normal creates the perfect breeding ground for inaction. What seems to be a creeping and marginal impact from upstart new entrants is at first easy to dismiss for a leadership team that doesn't want to think about what the long term might hold.

That lack of action can even seem like a winning strategy for a little while. Businesses congratulate themselves for not investing in new technologies or complex loyalty programmes and instead focusing on "the real basics of retailing, the things that matter to customers". For a short time, they even look more profitable than their competitors who are choosing to invest for change.

But then the story comes to an end, as what seemed to be a peripheral set of changes to a retail category becomes a tidal wave, and the brands which did not prepare get swept away.

So it might be understandable that retailers fail to grasp the need for change early enough, but it is not acceptable. Not if we are going to reinvent our business, side-step our new competitors and build customer relationships that will last for decades to come.

So as we move into Part 2, we'll shift from diagnosing the problem and its solutions towards a discussion about how we can really drive change. If you've finished Part 1 with a to-do list of things you'd like your colleagues to begin to grapple with, then you have made a great start. But now we need to consider the actions we can take to give those strategies the best chance of actually happening.

The way to do that is not gradual or subtle. It is to reboot your business. To engage people throughout the organisation in a conscious, explicit and honest process of assessing how the New Normal has changed the rules for you, and what you are going to do about it. Which aspects of your current business are valuable and important and worth doubling down on, and which need to be swept away. Which parts of your business are most at risk from disruptive new entrants and how you can embrace the opportunity to do that disruption yourself, never giving the new entrants a chance.

> **Building on the rules of the New Normal, in Part 2 we will explore a set of steps which can arm us to reinvent both our businesses and ourselves as business leaders. We'll explore examples of success and failure and learn the lessons from those, and we'll build our plan to reinvent our business.**

Part

2

A business plan for the
New Normal

Chapter

7

Building your plan

Welcome to Part 2. If you've read through Part 1 and devoted some time and thinking-space to the Action Planning exercises, you should have some ideas to help your business thrive in the New Normal. (And by the way, if you skipped over the exercises to save them for later, this is the time to go back and work through them. You'll find them helpful challenges to work through, and if you don't I'll buy you an ice cream to say sorry.)

As we discussed at the end of Part 1, it is easier to articulate the changes we want to make than it is to get them to actually happen. Over the course of Part 2 we'll try to address why that is, and make sure that our own strategies for the New Normal leap off the page and make a difference. We will do the following:

- Discover how to energise our teams.
- Make sure that our organisation has the skills it needs to effect change.
- Consider some powerful ways to get past 'Not Invented Here' and build momentum from early successes.
- Address the sometimes overwhelming task of bringing our shareholders, lenders and other stakeholders along with us.
- Put in place the measurements and incentives to ensure that the change we create is permanent, not temporary.

We need to start by pulling our conclusions from Part 1 together into the specific plan that is right for your business, in your sector, at this time. Part 1 offered many things that you *could* do. It's time to pull together your plan for what you *will* do.

Let's begin in a way you might not expect in a book with the word 'reinventing' in the title. We are going to consider how to preserve and protect the best of the business we have today while we also drive the change we need.

We touched on this before in Rule 4 when we talked about the role of the physical store in your business. The fact that many retail business models are being challenged and shattered in the New Normal does not mean that everything about those legacy businesses is bad. Indeed, as we've seen, many of the shiny pure-play new entrants in retailing now eye physical store estates with some envy, and at least one trillion-dollar company has built its success on marrying its shiny phones with an equally shiny store estate.

> **Our mission in reinventing our retail businesses is not to try to emulate the new competitors who have sprung up in the New Normal. It is to beat them.**

We beat our competitors by building the best of what they have into our business, but also by marrying that with the best of what we already have. Many of the most challenged retail businesses I can think of also have store locations, supplier relationships and thousands of colleagues who are expert in their products and loyal to the brand. That's a set of assets any new entrant would give their right mouse button for.

So our starting point in building our change plan is to consider the assets we already have and which we can deploy in the battle with our new competitors. But that requires something that will end up being a core ingredient of our reinvention plan: a huge dose of self-awareness and honest reflection.

A cautionary tale

Let's consider a salutary tale. We all remember the video rental shop. Walls and walls of VHS cassettes (and later DVDs), a display by the counter of a strange selection of really expensive snacks and a complicated mathematical formula outlining how many videos you could rent and for how long you could keep them.

I rather miss the thrill of heading to the rental shop hoping that they'd have the latest film in stock. I even miss the disappointment when they didn't, and we had to settle for another season of Star Trek, The Next Generation instead.

Whatever happened to video rental shops? Well, obviously, the world moved on.

With broadband connection to the internet, it gradually became possible to bypass the video rental shop entirely and deliver a film to our homes over the wire. Eventually we arrived where we are today: with the ability to buy or rent content online, choosing from a huge potential library, and watch what we've ordered instantly in high definition.

These new, easy, instant-access online video stores finally made the old business models redundant. One by one, at first gradually and then very rapidly indeed, a whole retail industry disappeared.

And the same thing has happened in other sectors where the New Normal has created new ways for consumers to consume. Amazon and the rise of the e-book may not have destroyed physical book-shops entirely, but very nearly. Indeed, large sections of the print media itself is now hanging on by a thread. Most local newspaper groups are struggling to survive and often do so, ironically, using revenue from online classified ads.

The really striking lesson for us, as we examine how to respond in our own businesses to the changing New Normal, is not that the video rental industry or the big bookstore chains have gone. That kind of change is all around us.

> **The real lesson comes from asking ourselves one key question: If the world was going to shift from rental stores to video stream-ing, why weren't the rental store companies themselves at the forefront of that change? Why aren't those brands today the giants of online movie services?**

Because after all, they started with all the advantages. At the point where video streaming over broadband was becoming possible, and the traditional video rental business was beginning to decline, consider the assets that the video rental companies would have been able to deploy in building a streaming business:

- They had all the relationships with movie distributors and content owners, and the credibility of many years of doing business with them.
- They had brands which were nationally and internationally recognisable and were associated with home entertainment in the consumers' mind.
- They had, in some form or other, billing systems and content databases already.
- They had a ready-made marketing channel – stores that millions of people walked into every week, staffed with colleagues who could sign those customers up to a new online service.
- And most critically, they knew us. They had massive databases of customers, knew the kinds of films we liked to watch, where we lived and how to get in touch with us.

For a traditional video rental company, the task of building an online streaming business would still have been difficult. They would have needed big investments in digital technologies, many of their historical agreements with the movie distributors would have needed to be re-written for the new world and the marketing investment involved in creating the new business would have been formidable.

But for a new entrant or start-up looking at this new emerging consumer market, all those things would have been true too, and they were starting with none of the advantages which the incumbent had.

And yet, despite starting with all the advantages, history shows us that the video streaming business has ended up being dominated by technology companies which hardly existed two decades ago and that the big brands which dominated traditional rental have by and large disappeared.

And this phenomenon is not limited to the video rental market. Online book retailing is not dominated by the brands that were big operators of bookshops before the internet arrived. Home delivery of groceries was pioneered in many countries not by existing supermarkets but by new entrants to the market.

And it is not just in physical retailing where innovation has turned out to be easier for new entrants than for incumbents. Look at internet giants like Facebook and Twitter buying up innovative start-ups like Foursquare and Instagram, often for billions of dollars.

How can it be that all the R&D might of a company like Facebook doesn't create a service allowing us to share photographs online, but a tiny start-up with a small team and some seed funding does it instead? The aggressive acquisition activity by the big internet giants shows us that they are hugely worried about being sidelined by innovations that they did not see coming, just as they themselves sidelined other industries when they arrived at the beginning of the New Normal. The change process challenging retail has not stopped and won't any time soon.

Why leaders often come last

So we've identified an interesting and persistent trend. When faced with game-changing innovation, historical leaders in a market often miss the opportunity to exploit their strengths and make this innovation their own. Instead, the change is often led by new entrants who are not encumbered by any of the history of the market. The established players are then faced with the choice of buying their way into the new market at a later stage if they can afford it or fading into obscurity if they can't.

Why is that? There is a clue in the last paragraph, and it is the word 'encumbered'.

All the assets we described the incumbent video rental operators as having can be looked at another way. The stores which generate the customer visits, the stock of DVDs on the shelves, the staff and the customer databases are all assets, for sure, but they are also the result of historical investments. Investments which need to be protected, and from which we need to earn a return for our shareholders.

There in a nutshell is the problem that holds back industry giants from embracing change and which often dooms them to the sidelines and to obscurity as new entrants and the New Normal change their world. The problem of legacy.

The things we've spent years building, the money we've invested into creating our business, the intellectual property that we've accumulated over time. All of these represent things that it is perfectly natural for us to want to protect and nurture. It is human nature when faced with a set of legacy investments like this that we organise our thinking around them. As retail businesses around the world faced the growth of e-commerce, it was completely natural that much of the boardroom debate that resulted was framed around how to protect their stores. How to keep customers coming to the physical store and fend off the traditional business from the attack of new entrants and innovation.

The sunk cost fallacy

Economists have a term for this. They call it the 'sunk cost fallacy'. Money we've already spent, and can't recoup, is gone. It is illogical for us to base our future decisions on the money we've already spent. We should focus instead on the costs and benefits that we can alter in the future.

Consider an example. I've bought an expensive and non-refundable train ticket to go to the country this weekend. The weather report now says that instead of a weekend in the sunshine, it is actually going to be cold and wet, and I find that one of the attractions I wanted to visit while I was there will be closed for a few days.

There are many factors which influence whether I still choose to go on my trip or not. But the fact that I've already bought my train ticket should, logically, make no difference. After all, I've spent the money on the ticket whether I go or not. There is nothing I can do about that now, and going for a miserable weekend in the rain just because I already have a ticket makes no sense, does it?

But of course I go anyway. Behavioural economists have regularly observed that as humans we base our decisions on sunk costs all the time. It might be irrational to base a future decision on past spending that we can't get back, but it is deeply human. We've all felt the pull to do something, or go somewhere, that no longer makes sense just because if we don't, then our earlier decisions look silly. If I don't go the country, and I waste my train ticket, then I was stupid to buy it in the first place, wasn't I?

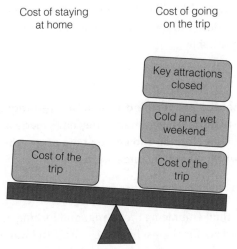

Cost of staying at home

Cost of going on the trip

Key attractions closed

Cold and wet weekend

Cost of the trip

Cost of the trip

Figure 7.1 The cost sunk fallacy

If this kind of irrational decision-making results in us having a miserable weekend in the rain, then that's just our tough luck. But the impact of the sunk cost fallacy is much greater than that, because it doesn't just affect the decisions we make as individual consumers. It also dominates the formation of business strategies, even for very large companies.

This is never clearer than when boards of directors worry about protecting and earning a return from the historical investments the company has made. If you have a lot of money tied up in a chain of shops, but everyone now buys your product online, then you have a challenge about what to do with those shops. You might be able to reposition them as customer-recruitment or customer-service outlets. You might be able to sell them to someone else who has a use for them. Or you might face a painful decision about closing them altogether.

But whatever you do with those shops makes no difference at all to the other decision in front of you. Do you follow your customers online and serve them in the way they now want to be served, or do you leave that changed market to someone else to profit from?

Put that way, the decision seems obvious, but over the years far too many businesses have shied away from new channels and new technologies. They'll tell themselves (and their shareholders) that they are doing so because the new channels are unproven, small or unprofitable.

> **Many businesses are terrified of admitting to themselves that some of the historical investments they have made are no longer right for the New Normal, and some of the assets they have built up are not worth what they once were.**

Rather than embracing the change and locking up the new emerging markets for themselves, they circle the wagons around their historical business with the inevitable long-term result.

So what can we do?

There is no point pretending that turning a long-established industry leader to face into the changed world of the New Normal is somehow easy. If your sales channels have become less relevant, or your factory has been outpaced by new developments in manufacturing technology, or your customer service model is being challenged by new and lower cost ways of solving customers' problems online, then you have a real challenge on your hands.

But it is illogical, and ultimately futile, to pretend that change isn't happening just to try to protect legacy assets. Instead, the smart approach is to split the problem into two different questions:

- What is the best way we can embrace the New Normal in our industry to prevent new entrants from entering the market and earning profits which we are better placed than them to earn? Which aspects of our history legacy business are really going to help us to achieve that?
- Meanwhile, what is the best way we can utilise, repurpose, exit or otherwise deal with parts of our business which are no longer valuable to our customers?

Each of those is a difficult question, and worth a serious discussion around the board table. But the answer to the second question is not to pretend that the first one doesn't exist. That way leads to the video store.

So if our objective is to work out which aspects of our business are genuinely going to be strengths as we implement our new strategy, how best can we do that?

The answer, of course, is to start with the customer. They, and they alone, can decide whether an offering is one they will choose to pay for. Only the collective response of customers to a new strategy matters, and it is our honest understanding of this response which will enable us to shed our sunk cost fallacy and assess our business objectively.

That understanding might be intuitive and come from your team's ability to get into the minds of your customers and see the world their way. Or it might require the kind of customer research techniques that we've already discussed in Part 1 and which we will come across again next. Either way, however, this challenge of assessing our own strengths and weaknesses through the eyes of our customer is essential.

A four-step process to generate a strategy for the New Normal

Whichever route you choose to gather your customer feedback, I suggest the following four-stage structure for a serious assessment of your strengths and weaknesses in the New Normal. It is the best way you can build on the rules in Part 1 in a way that is specific and relevant to your business.

1. How is the experience your customers expect in your sector changing in the New Normal?
   - This might be as simple as they now expect to search and buy online as well as in store.
   - Or it might be that your service is being dis-intermediated and broken into smaller bits by new entrants.
   - Or it might be that the balance of what customers are willing to pay you for is changing as they demand more personalised or customised experiences from you.

- Customers might have new alternatives, such as other places to buy the products you sell, or even entirely different products that satisfy their underlying need. Think of the way that watching a film at home is different to going to the cinema but still arguably a substitute for it sometimes.

- Indeed, any of the changes we discussed in Part 1 might be impacting your customers, and usually several will be at once.

2. Given that, what changes do you need to make in your business in order to meet and exceed that customer demand?

- You might need to reshape your offering, redesign your retail layout, revise your pricing strategies, or make one of a number of other changes in order to 'lean in' to that new customer reality rather than denying it.

- This, of course, begins to become the skeleton of the new things you need to do in order to create your strategy for the New Normal.

3. As you do that, how can you leverage your historical assets to deliver a service for your customers that is even better than your new entrant competitors?

- If customers want to buy online, you need to sell online of course. But if you have a physical store estate too, how can that augment the online shopping experience? Click and collect services and returns to stores are good examples, but can you think of more?

- If your competitors are supermarkets or online giants selling your products alongside thousands of others, then you have some tough price competition ahead. But how can the expertise of your colleagues in-store bring to life curated sets of products, bundles and other recommendations that add value to customers. How can your long-standing relationship with suppliers allow you to stock rare, scarce or customised product variants?

- Going through this process will add the second element of your strategy: the ways in which you can use your historical strengths to out-do and out-compete those new entrants.

4. Finally, what aspects of your historical business are obstacles that need to be overcome to deliver on that strategy?

- The classic legacy burden for many retailers is IT systems, of course. But just as challenging can be cost models that leave you uncompetitive versus new entrants or established working practices which are no longer appropriate in the New Normal but are "just the way we've always done it" (remember those insurance companies).

- You may also find that some aspects of your business which can be used to great effect also need to change a lot. Your stores might be a multi-channel asset against online-only competitors, but they might need significant refurbishment to achieve that, and you might need far fewer of them too.

- What can you do to work around, alleviate or eliminate those burdens? There is a significant challenge here for many retailers. There is a long list of brands, for instance, that have embarked on lengthy, expensive and distinctly old-school IT projects in order to build their multi-channel capabilities only to find that a new entrant with an IT team of ten does the same thing in a weekend and on a shoestring. We'll talk some more later about how to avoid that.

- This is the most difficult stage of the exercise, but coming up with an effective plan to side-step legacy barriers to the delivery of your strategy is critical. It will require careful stakeholder management (which we will also discuss later) but is quite literally mission-critical.

So there you have a four-stage process. Starting with the customer, working out how their needs are changing and what we need to do about it, coming up with ways that our historical strengths can turbo-charge that new strategy, and also coming up with ways to avoid being slowed down or weighed down by our legacy.

Figure 7.2 The four-stage strategy process

A worked example

To bring all of that to life, let's consider a worked example. This might be similar to your own situation, but even if it's not, I hope it gives you some food for thought.

Retailer X has 500 small stores around the UK and more in some other countries. It has a strong position in a specialist sector, with great supplier relationships, some real product differentiation and a loyal and enthusiastic colleague base in store. But despite all of that, internet pure-plays have made persistent in-roads into X's market share. Some of that has been Amazon and other multi-sector giants, but small players too have sprung up, often growing out of websites and discussion forums for fans of the products that X sells. Now, even the supermarkets and discounters are getting in on the action.

What can X do to protect and grow its position? Well, Part 1 generated a long list of opportunities. The management team can look to increase the pace of product innovation to see off those competitors for whom this sector is a small niche that they won't invest in. It can get more nimble at bundling products together and using strategic pricing as a weapon. It has a huge opportunity to use its customer database and the customer knowledge that springs from that database to grow its business with each customer by treating them as individuals with different product and service needs.

How can X deploy its strengths to make those strategies more likely to succeed? Well, its strong brand gives it a great platform to bring new product bundles to market. Its customer data makes it possible to build membership, repeat purchases and even subscription offerings for its most valuable customers. Most importantly, its high-street locations and brilliant teams can create demand for its products by creating events and promotions for passers-by to discover.

So what's the problem? Which aspects of X's business might get in the way of that? Well, it has a lot of stores and times have been hard for the last couple of years, so they are in need of investment. They aren't necessarily the vibrant product showcases that our strategy calls for. Tough times have also led to hours in store being cut back and valuable colleagues have left the business. X's IT systems are also decidedly last-decade, and so launching new and more complex commercial offerings is tougher than it looks. And its website, installed by an expensive systems integrator, is OK but no more than that. It works, but doesn't really integrate into store operations to allow really multi-channel projects to fly.

Does that all sound familiar?

As we've reviewed so far, the next step for X is two-fold. On the one hand, it needs to lay out the plan to bring its strengths to bear and deliver on a strategy for the New Normal. That is not negotiable, since it is the only way to prevent death by a thousand competitor cuts.

But in parallel, it needs to find ways to by-pass its legacy issues. It might need to close some stores, as painful as that is, to free up capital to reposition those which remain as brand hubs. It might need to take an entirely different approach to IT, perhaps starting again with a more modern and web-centric architecture.

And whatever it does, it needs to pass the customer test. Is it creating products and services that consumers react positively to and which will win market share, and is it doing so on a cost base which allows it to earn a return at the same time?

Bringing it together

None of that is simple, but the four-question process is an incredibly powerful exercise to do.

There are two reasons for that, I find. The first is obvious. In answering the four questions we are beginning to develop our own strategy for coping with the New Normal.

A lot of the action planning exercises in Part 1 will have given you ideas for strategic responses. This process should bring those together into a coherent whole that builds from the business you have today.

But the second reason is important too. More than anything, strategic change is about people change. Some of the barriers to survival in the New Normal are in people's heads ('not invented here' or 'if I just wait things will go back to normal'). And indeed, most of the solutions to the challenge are in people's heads too, in their product knowledge, customer relationships and passion for your brand.

We are going to have to change the hearts and minds of thousands of colleagues in hundreds of locations in order to make our strategy stick. Much of the rest of Part 2 is devoted to that challenge. But understanding the real strengths of our business and the assets we bring to the competitive battle allows us to commence the hearts and minds programme with something which I have repeatedly found to be among the most powerful things a leader can bring to a business – respect.

By acknowledging the skills and expertise of our people and the history of the business, you can begin to bring people on a journey to a new way of doing business. I've seen too many strategy programmes implicitly start with "Everything here is rubbish, we should be more like that new digital business over there". And immediately fail as a result.

> **Show some respect to the business you have today and the people in it are more likely to help you build the business you need for tomorrow.**

Now, we've seen in this chapter the importance of building our strategy on sound customer feedback. This is just one example of the oldest adage in business: You get what you measure. If we are to reinvent our business, we need to reinvent our KPIs too, and that's what we'll do next.

Chapter

You get what you measure

We have just talked about the importance of using customer feedback as the filter for our strategic choices. There is no point putting a new strategy in place if it doesn't create products and service experiences that customers value.

Here's a simple way of expressing that goal. We are trying to make sure that people enjoy being our customers so much that they choose to come back again and again, and even tell their friends how terrific we are.

The highest prize of the New Normal is engagement – becoming a business that people really want to associate with.

When switching between brands is easy and it is simple to compare prices and features, it matters more than ever that our brands stand out from the crowd. As customers have become better informed but also much more able to share suggestions, ideas, recommendations and complaints online, our reputations play a bigger and bigger role in whether we succeed against our competitors or not.

As luck would have it, there is a measure of whether we are succeeding. Net promoter score (NPS) asks recent customers a very simple question: Would you recommend this brand to your friends? They give an answer between 0 and 10, and the formula then processes that into a single number in the following way. Anyone giving you a 9 or 10 is deemed a promoter; anyone giving a score between 0 and 6 is a detractor; and anyone giving 7 or 8 is a passive.

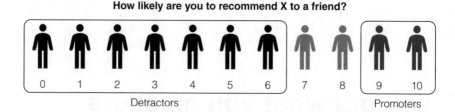

How likely are you to recommend X to a friend?

Detractors — 0 1 2 3 4 5 6 | 7 8 | 9 10 — Promoters

NPS = % of promoters – % of detractors

Figure 8.1 The NPS equation

Your NPS score is simply the proportion of promoters minus the proportion of detractors. The passives in the middle are simply ignored as they were trying to be polite when they completed the survey but were clearly not passionate enough in either direction for their view to impact the score.

An NPS score can therefore be a negative number (as much as –100 if all your customers are detractors, in which case I'd suggest you have bigger priorities than reading this book) and can go up to +100 if everything is perfect.

Why is NPS a useful KPI?

The theory behind NPS is fascinating. By using 'Would you recommend this' as the question, we raise the bar significantly on our measurement. Simply asking if I enjoyed the service or would rate it highly is one thing, but for me to actually recommend a brand to a friend is a big deal. By doing so, I'm associating myself with the brand and I will not do that if I have any doubts about it at all. Similarly, by analysing the polar results (the very high and very low scores) we are pulling out the really important views – the people who are actually likely to make that recommendation or, on the contrary, the people who feel so negatively about us that they are likely to tell their friends that too.

Why might NPS be unhelpful?

NPS can also be a controversial measure. There is no doubt that as it has become more widely used it is also starting to get 'gamed'. Charles Goodhart coined his famous law in the 1970s and it still holds good today. Once a measure becomes a target, it ceases to be an effective measure because the people we are holding to account for the measure will start to find ways to make the number move in the right direction, and not all of which will be the consequences we intended.

I experienced a terrific example of Goodhart's Law being applied to NPS when a service engineer from my broadband provider visited my house. After finishing his repair, he gave me a big speech about the fact that I would get a text later asking how satisfied I was with his visit, and to be careful not to give a 7 or 8 because those didn't count, and only a 9 or 10 would earn him his bonus.

In addition to being 'game-able', NPS is also a very fragile measure. If you make a very slight change to the research methodology (asking other questions as well as the NPS one, for example, or changing the channels through which customers can respond), then you can see the numbers shift wildly. It is, for the same reason, hard to get a robust measure of NPS for your competitors using the same methodology (and therefore generating comparable data) as you use for yourself.

We, however, are running businesses, not research institutes. We aren't trying to write learned papers about our industries, we are trying to win business from our competitors. And in that practical world, there is no better measure of whether we are getting it right at the front line than tracking whether or not our customers feel inclined to recommend us to their friends.

I've used granular, outlet-by-outlet measurement of NPS in several retail and hospitality businesses. In every case, there was an element of gaming. One region ends up complaining that another region is somehow cheating because it shows a higher NPS. Also, in every case I've seen how fragile the measure can be to changes in method. There is no point comparing your NPS score of 40 with a *Harvard Business Review* article that talks about an industry leader having a score of 70 when you can tweak your questionnaire slightly and shift the number by 20 points in one direction or another.

So what's the point of spending all of the time and money gathering the thousands of data points every week that are necessary to produce a store-by-store NPS score? There are two.

> **Using NPS as a scorecard gets the whole organisation talking about it.**

A business discussing what it might mean to delight a customer enough that they want to recommend it to their friends is a business investing its time wisely. Senior management interrogating why the numbers have gone up (or down) in a particular week can prompt valuable discussions about what is going on in the market, what competitors are up to and how customers are feeling. Unlike many financial measures, NPS feels like an outward-facing and customer-facing measure. Too much time in many businesses is spent chasing largely internal-looking figures like costs and margins. It does us good to balance those critical KPIs with some that get us thinking about our markets.

How to improve your NPS score

The second benefit of using NPS is the big one and it follows along from getting the business talking about the measure.

Sooner or later, once you start producing league tables of performance, weekly reports and all the other materials that go along with a new KPI, someone will ask the magic question.

> **What can we actually do to make the number go up?**

For a smart business, this question is the beginning of an amazing journey. There are two equally powerful ways of answering the question, which together can be a terrific catalyst for organisational change. One is to answer the question from the outside in, starting with your customers and your front-line teams. The other is to answer it from the inside out, using the data and some analysis. Let's consider these in turn.

Finding out the key things that drive NPS in your business from the outside in is a terrific way to connect the organisation to the real world outside the office or the store. A wide range of research companies are all too keen to help with the process, and I've seen and participated in several different techniques including:

- The traditional focus group, where a small group of customers talk about your industry, the brands in it and their experience of your products and services. It is often possible to watch these from behind a one-way mirror and I strongly recommend it, particularly for head office and senior teams who might not be talking to live customers on a daily basis.

- Even more interesting is the interactive focus group or 'customer closeness' session where a group of people from the company work with a group of customers in facilitated workshops.

- Taking customer closeness to its logical conclusion is ethnographic research, where you visit customers in their homes, go on accompanied shopping trips with them and really see your brand through their eyes.

All these tools can provide rich insights into the aspects of your service that really drive positive and negative reactions from customers. So, however, does another set of discussions – those with your own front-line colleagues. A set of workshops dotted around your key trading territories where you bring teams together from both head office and the front line serves a neat dual purpose. It demonstrates to those colleagues who deal with customers every day that senior teams are interested in the experience the brand is delivering and want to hear their point of view, while at the same time generating practical insights about customers too.

All of this data-gathering is what researchers would call qualitative in contrast to quantitative research where large-scale surveys return tables of numbers. That's just as it should be. My experience is that small-scale qualitative research generates much more powerful feedback than an anonymous survey. Plus there is the added cultural benefit of having people from around the business actually spending time with customers, generating their own experiences and anecdotes that they can use in the course of their roles. In any case, surveys of customers about what drives great experiences tend to generate fairly bland answers, usually of the 'make your product cheaper' variety.

Building a 'drivers' model

Of course, we do want some hard data to go along with our insights, but we have a much better source of that. We have the data from our NPS questions themselves, and the opportunity that gives us to take an inside-out view of the world.

It is rare that an NPS survey just asks the one single recommendation question. To be accurate, the survey should have as few questions as possible and not turn into a 45-minute 'What did you think of the window display' kind of questionnaire. Those turn customers off and only particularly opinionated (and largely unrepresentative) customers will complete them. Nonetheless, there is usually room for half a dozen or so additional questions and the most obvious ones to include will be those about major aspects of your product or service experience. For a retailer, these might be questions about the tidiness and attractiveness of the store, the attitude of the staff, the availability of product and so on.

Once you've built up a database of thousands of these answers, it becomes possible for the statisticians to do their work. The task is this: For which of these extra questions do the answers most closely correlate with the overall NPS score? Which of the things we are questioning, therefore, can we surmise might be key drivers of the recommendation decision for customers? There are a range of powerful analytical techniques which your team, or specialist consultants, can use to pull these key drivers out of your data.

The power of hello

The answers can be surprising. In two separate retail businesses where I've done this, the number 1 driver of NPS scores was the same. It was whether or not when the customer first walked into the store, someone looked up, smiled and said hello.

It turned out that that initial split-second experience, our first impression as it were, drove everything else.

The customer who had walked in with a complaint at least had someone to listen to them. The customer who had walked in uncertain and with questions could get them answered. And the customer who didn't want to interact with anyone and knew exactly what they were there to buy at least had the warm sense of being somewhere they were welcomed.

That all makes sense, but it is not necessarily what either organisation would have picked out as an answer before the exercise began. What about the expensive 'point of sale' we've put all around the store? What about the merchandising and product displays? What about the logo? It's not that those things didn't matter at all, but for a real customer visiting a real store more human things were more important.

Five key steps to using NPS well

I heartily recommend that you embrace NPS and introduce (or reintroduce) it through the business, making sure to do the following:

1. Invest in measuring it often enough and granularly enough to be able to get a figure for each store or outlet, or for each product line, every week.

2. Create and foster a debate around your business about NPS and how to improve it, using small group discussions to generate real actions.

3. Invest in a customer closeness programme to ensure that (in particular) those executives with important decisions to make, but who don't see customers all the time, get enough customer face-time to be able to form their own views on what drives NPS.

4. Do the analytics on the NPS surveys and associated questions to develop some hypotheses about the key drivers of NPS.

5. And above all, socialise all of this loudly and often around the business. Don't just measure NPS, but be seen to care about it.

In the long run, however, I will also make a prediction about the outcome of this process. The key drivers of NPS will of course vary from industry to industry and even from brand to brand. The detail of your outcomes from the process we've laid out here will be unique to you.

> **But at their heart, most of the key drivers of NPS in your business will be about people.**

The NPS drivers might be very directly about your people and how they interact with your customers, like my story of the power of hello.

They might also be indirectly about your people. In the cinema business, for example, the number 2 driver of NPS (after hello) was whether the toilets were clean when the customer visited. Now every cinema or restaurant business will have a toilet cleaning rota, but whether it actually happens, and happens on time and effectively, is about the morale and motivation of the team working in the cinema, and the morale and motivation of their supervisors and managers. So even something so practical is really about people.

NPS and the New Normal

These emerging insights about what really drives NPS, which I've seen across several industries, point to an underlying contradiction in the New Normal, and one which we can use to our advantage.

On the one hand, the growth of internet selling, price comparison websites, review and ratings sites, plus all the other changes we've seen so far have served to make it easier for new entrants by somehow distancing consumers from real brand experiences. When every possible supplier for a product is just a two-line listing in a Google search, and when the easiest way to compare them is on a price comparison site there seems to be less room for differentiation, customer service and other aspects of brand to allow one business to do better than another. It is this mechanical logic of the New Normal which leads to price erosion, products being sold at cost and physical retail outlets being gradually replaced by online warehouses.

And yet, when asked to rate experiences and recommend brands (including the brands which only exist as pure-play online retailers), customers reach for the emotional and the human aspects of the interaction. The greeting, helpfulness and manner of the sales assistant, the attitude of the delivery drivers or service engineers, the experience of talking to someone in the call centre – these are consistently the things that help us decide whether a brand is for us or not.

Even with a brand where there is virtually no human interaction, the same thing holds true. Listen to people talk about Amazon and they will quite quickly start talking about how customer-friendly the returns policy is. That's another non-human interaction, but in the mind of the consumer it represents helpfulness and thoughtfulness.

The implications of this insight are profound. Of course, every business has always talked about the importance of its people, and most businesses of any scale have some set of words that are designed to govern and guide behaviours across the organisation in the form of a mission statement, a list of values and so on.

But despite that, the real focus in many businesses from an operational point of view has been process compliance, cost control and the achievement of commercial targets like sales conversion and add-on sales attachment rates. Now most management teams have been sincere at some level about the importance of culture, values and behaviours across the organisation, but again from an operational point of view most attention even in this area has gone into compliance – weeding out employee behaviours which are not acceptable, for instance.

The New Normal reality, however, is that it is the willingness of local teams in your depot, store, restaurant or service organisation to go the extra mile for your customers which is the thing they will remember and tell their friends about.

Indeed, if you want your brand to be judged on something other than the two-line Google description and an internet price comparison, these real human drivers of NPS and recommendations are your most powerful weapons. Often, they are the core aspect of your historic assets that you will use to differentiate yourselves if you follow the process we have laid out.

Using NPS to drive real change

To achieve that, we need to take the mission and values statements off the wall and make them an everyday reality. In particular, we need to move our people processes from ones focused on compliance and weeding out bad behaviour into ones focused on discovering, promoting and creating excellence in delighting customers. There are a number of techniques that leadership teams can use to achieve that:

- **Lead by example**: Every time I talk to CEOs and boards who lead organisations with high NPS scores and brands which are really differentiated on customer service, I hear the same story. That it is the example set by the leadership team which is the biggest signal to the rest of the organisation of the kind of behaviours that will get rewarded.

- **Review individual customer complaints:** Trace them through to their root causes and use that to drive change.

- **Work on your own front line:** Spend enough time experiencing what it means to work there (and be seen by your people doing so).

- **Experience your own customer service**: I've seen too many businesses where senior staff never need to call the call centre because they have an internal hotline they can use instead. This can get to such an extreme that for one giant brand a big problem with customer service response times only became apparent to the board when it was in the press.

- **Design the organisation with the customer in mind:** Do your first-line managers spend their time coaching and motivating their people or are they hidden in a back room doing paperwork? If it's the latter, it is probably paperwork that the corporate centre insists that they do, and it is almost certainly not for the benefit of your customers.

- **Train for success:** It's almost a vintage joke now that corporations cut training first when times get tough, but as much of a stereotype as that might be it still happens more often than it should. And even when we train, are we training simply on the mechanics of processing tasks, or are we training to get the outcome that we want. If you are a restaurant business, then the manner and presentation skills of your servers will be a huge constituent part of your NPS score. If your induction process for new hires is simply to teach them the computer systems and other operational basics, then you are entirely at the mercy of their natural abilities when they talk to your guests. If, on the other hand, you invest in showing them what great looks like, you might just make a difference to that all-important customer recommendation.

In general, a powerful review for a leadership team to do is to unpack the ingredients of NPS, the things that will really drive a recommendation from a delighted customer and consider how to build a set of processes and measurements which will ensure those things happen every time. That might extend to the way products and services are designed and to the hiring and training policies of the business but it also might change pricing policies, marketing messages and more.

But there is a danger here. That all-important initial hello to each customer offers a really good example. Simply mandating that a corporately selected phrase is used as a greeting every time a customer walks through the door is obviously not going to win market share. Such a phrase will quickly sound tired and clichéd, and your own teams will become sick of saying it, which in turn will become obvious to the customer.

We know what our customers really mean when they talk about the power of hello. It's not a specific form of words they are looking for, but a warm and positive greeting from someone who is pleased to see them and is there to help.

The business change programme, which is designed to get real and effective customer greetings to happen, will be a huge and all-consuming challenge precisely because we are not looking for a one-size-fits-all answer.

> **We are looking to ensure that our front-line teams are interested enough, motivated and trained to deliver a great greeting, and that they understand the strategic importance of doing so.**

Simplifying the task into a simple script will never achieve that goal. Only a profound discussion across the business and a set of meaningful changes to people policies will do so.

But the prize is worth it. If you are lucky enough to have real people talking to your customers every day, unlike those poor online retailers who only see clicks, and you are skilled enough to turn those customer interactions into brand-enhancing moments, then you have uncovered a competitive weapon against the low-cost warehouses.

Beyond NPS to other important KPIs

If NPS, and the associated measures of customer experience which flow from it, are important KPIs to orient your business around, it is because they are customer-facing. There are some other directions we should face too, as we pull together a well-rounded set of KPIs to focus the organisation around.

One we've discussed already is the KPI that springs up from facing towards our competitors in the marketplace – market share. As you saw in Part 1, a clear measure of market share is a fantastic way to focus your commercial teams on whether they are winning or losing ground versus your rivals.

There are, however, some important things to get right about your use of the market share KPI:

- Sourcing any market share information at all can be tricky. I've seen retail businesses with incredibly granular market share data allowing a store-by-store and day-by-day analysis of what was going on in the high street. There are plenty of other sectors, however, where hardly any useful share information is available at all. But the power of market share is such that it is well worth putting some real thought into how you can source some data, sometimes even taking a cross-industry approach through a trade association or other body.

- The frequency and granularity of that data makes a big difference to how valuable it is. A quarterly countrywide measure is interesting, but is only ever a backward-looking number, whereas a weekly figure becomes a vital part of your trading cycle, influencing promotional decisions and providing valuable competitor intelligence.

- However outward-focused and action-oriented market share is, it is also only one part of the story of your overall sales performance. The other is the rate of growth or decline of your market itself. Don't be fooled into feeling too smug about strong market share in a declining market. The market will win in the end and now is the time to consider how you can expand, redefine or otherwise reshape your market so that you are fishing in a more attractive pond.

Bringing it together

This pair of KPIs – NPS and market share – represent a powerful combination of outward-facing measures that can orient a retail business towards its customers and its competitors. My experience has been that introducing them, or increasing their importance, in a consumer business can have a transformational impact.

There are many other KPIs we need to run our business, such as measuring financial performance, stock levels and sell-through, store-level performance and policy compliance. But I'm willing to bet that you have plenty of those already. A surprising number of retail businesses, however, have managed to get away with a weekly and monthly trading pack that has lots of information about stock turn, hours worked versus hours budgeted and average basket size but nothing at all about how customers felt about the business and very little about what competitors did.

In the New Normal, the old pack won't get us where we need to go whereas the new outward-looking KPIs we've discussed here are essential. But they will only help if they are the opening gambit in a much bigger change programme. As we saw with NPS, the point is not to *force* everyone in the store to say hello to customers, but to engineer a business full of people who *want* to say hello to customers. That means that the next phases of bringing our strategy into action are about our people, ensuring that they have the knowledge and skills to survive in the New Normal and are active, engaged co-creators of our strategy with a vested interest in making it work.

That's where we'll go next, and we'll start with taking that challenge ourselves.

Chapter

9

Building your digital skills

Picture the scene. A group of business leaders get together to discuss strategic and political issues of the day, perhaps hosted by a headhunter or consulting firm. Someone around the table refers to a news item from earlier that day. "Oh", you say, "I never read the news." That doesn't sound very plausible, does it?

How about a different scenario where the discussion turns to returns on investment for some project or another. "Actually," you say, "I can't really do sums like that." Also not sounding good?

And yet, it is still somehow acceptable to say that we don't really do social media or don't have a clue how websites work. Within a few years, however, admitting to this degree of digital ignorance is likely to be as embarrassing (and career-limiting) as admitting to illiteracy or innumeracy would be today.

There is a good reason for that.

> **In the New Normal, a good understanding of how technology has changed and evolved, coupled with an equally good understanding of what that means for how consumers live their lives, is an increasingly vital tool for the business executive.**

Consider what we miss if we are not as digitally literate as we are simply literate:

- We will make decisions about investing in websites and other digital technologies without really understanding what we are investing in, and therefore profoundly ill-equipped to choose between different strategies.

- We will make branding and marketing decisions without a good intuitive understanding of how customers really form and share impressions of brands in the New Normal, with the consequent danger that we will push on with expensive media investments like TV advertising long after they have stopped being relevant to our consumers.
- We will fail to connect our online and offline businesses in ways that matter to consumers and really differentiate us from our competitors.
- We will miss trends and emerging technologies as they arise, with the consequent danger that we will simply jump unthinkingly on emerging bandwagons without properly understanding what we are getting into.
- We will miss out on a terrific channel to connect with our customers and gain a window into how they see and use our brands.

If these sound like distant or theoretical issues, don't be fooled. All of them are happening in businesses right now and have been for as long as the New Normal has been emerging.

Investing while blindfolded

Take investment in technology, for example. The challenge facing senior management teams and boards when choosing technology investments is that, particularly in older legacy businesses, an odd organisational situation has grown up. Of course, the team is advised by a CTO or other technology leader, and they in turn will have project managers, business analysts and technology strategists advising them.

Strangely enough, however, many of these senior technology people have little experience in new digital technologies themselves. They may have come up through the project-management route and therefore have excellent process skills but less front-line technology knowledge. Or they may be technologists who have developed their skills and expertise in the legacy financial and operational systems that your business is built on rather than the world of the web.

The result of this organisational situation is that there are often many layers of management between the ultimate decision-makers and the first person in the chain who really knows the various technology options at first hand. Even worse, quite often the first people in the chain who really know the technology being discussed are in the vendor companies themselves, or in consulting firms which may therefore have interests which are not aligned with yours.

The consequences of this expertise gap can be darkly comic. I recall an example where the leaders of one business wanted a change on a web page which, if you knew the HTML language in which websites are written, you would know required the addition of one single character to the code (a #, as it happens). By the time, however, the various layers of well-intentioned but under-informed business and technology people had turned the request into a work request and then into a functional requirements document, and also done all the other administrative steps in the process, not only had weeks already passed but the sombre answer was that the change would cost tens of thousands and take six months to deliver.

The same consequences can also be seriously business-critical. Many retail businesses over the last five years have been persuaded that the right way to upgrade poor websites to good ones was to implement giant (and proprietary) web-retailing platforms provided by global technology companies and implemented by layers of specialist consultants. The almost invariable result was a change programme costing millions and taking years, which in the end delivers a set of functionalities which smaller and more nimble digital competitors had already superseded. In at least one case, the bill for this kind of bloated web project was part of the reason why a retail business ultimately went into administration.

Equally vital strategic decisions in other parts of a company's operations are much less likely to go so spectacularly wrong. If that same retail business was evaluating a decision about where to open new stores, or about a new design of shop-fit, or about new warehousing systems and processes, the team around the table would be much better equipped to spot a mistake before it was made.

The experts around the table on those decisions would generally have more direct personal expertise, and the rest of the team evaluating the options would have the benefit of experience and instinct to guide them. When making decisions about digital technologies, however, those instincts are expensively missing.

Buzz-word bingo

It isn't just in capital investment decisions that this experience gap can hurt us. If you watch TV and movies the old-fashioned way but want to reach a target audience which is under 25, how can you make media-buying or marketing decisions? If you buy through the sales channels you've always done, how can you spot challenging new trends? How many supermarket executives spent so much time visiting theirs and their competitors' supermarkets that they didn't spot small-format discount players emerging until it was too late? How many hours in board meetings have been wasted by people throwing around buzz-word terms like 'big data' or 'segmentation' or 'multi-channel' without really having much idea of what those terms mean?

It is easy now with the benefit of hindsight to ridicule businesses which in the late 1990s added 'dot com' to their company names to try to sound more hip and with it (although a lot of people have forgotten that such ridiculous tactics actually worked for a worryingly long time). But take a look around now at the blizzard of press releases about the latest technology trends and you'll see the same thing happening – trendy terms being used by people with very little understanding of what they mean, to try to excite or bamboozle others with even less idea.

Consider these headlines:

- We've applied the latest in Artificial Intelligence techniques to deliver for our customers.
- We are pioneering the use of blockchain to revolutionise our logistics eco-system.
- We've introduced hackathons to turbo-charge our innovation.

Any idea what those mean? Me neither. Did I make them up or steal them from LinkedIn? Bet you can't tell.

All of these technology terms contain the seeds of the real change in the New Normal that could either revolutionise our business or allow a new entrant to destroy it. The challenge is to make the right investment decisions at the right time.

> **It is our responsibility as business leaders to ensure that our skills (and those of the people in our teams) are fit for the task in front of us.**

In the New Normal, that set of skills has broadened. We need all the expertise we've always had. As you've seen it is often that historical skillset which can be used to differentiate our business from the shiny online new entrants to our markets. But we also need to have at least enough familiarity with the language, technologies and behaviours of the New Normal to be able to make sensible decisions about where to invest and how to compete.

As a starting point, here is a set of questions to ask of yourself and your management team:

1. Do you know, at a high level, how a website works?

2. Do you know what customer data your business gathers, how it stores it and how a data query might work? In other words, what kind of questions can you ask of your data?

3. Have you ever looked at the Google Analytics (or other analysis tool) page for your website, and if you did, would you know what you are looking at?

4. Have you ever sent a Snapchat, a Whatsapp message or posted a picture on Instagram? For a bonus point, are you aware of how brands can advertise and connect with consumers through those and other social channels?

5. What KPIs do you use for your social media channels and how much money do you invest in them?

6. How do you track the way your customers use your channels? A retailer will typically know the sales made in store and on the web but will often not know how many of the sales in-store started with a research trip to the website, or vice versa. How do your channels interrelate for your customers?

7. How familiar are you with issues of cybersecurity and data protection and what those mean for your business?

8. Do you know what Artificial Intelligence (or more realistically the subset of AI techniques called machine learning) could do for your business?

These might seem like quite technical questions for a non-technical business leader to be able to answer. Consider, however, the comparison to more traditional business learning points. A good business leader will have walked (and probably worked in) their warehouse. They will spend time in stores or restaurants or other outlets where relevant, will know how to work the tills in those locations and will have worked shifts to make sure they have talked to customers and experienced business processes from a user's perspective.

All those experiences will translate into knowledge that is directly useful in business decision-making. When changing business processes or launching new ones, when evaluating new product lines or withdrawing old ones, good business leaders will draw on their own experiences at the sharp end, as well as the data being presented.

Many of the decisions we face, however, in adapting our businesses to deal with the New Normal require equivalent front-end experiences in areas which are new to us. Without the equivalent personal experiences, management teams have to lean unquestioningly on the advice from their own technology teams or (even worse) vendors of services.

I've seen retail boards forensically analyse a single new site opening based on personal experience of the town where the site is proposed to be and on a deep detailed understanding of the trading performance of sites in nearby locations. But I've seen the same retail boards nod through huge investments in digital technology without applying any of the same rigour, because the IT department said so. That disparity in the depth and detail of decision-making cannot lead to good outcomes.

An action plan for learning

Assuming that you come up short in some of these areas, what can you do about it? It is time to make the most profitable digital investment of all and spend some time learning about the tools and techniques your online rivals take for granted. Here are seven learning goals that can transform an organisation:

1. Learn to build a website. Yes, that sounds like a scary objective, but there are digital agencies and training shops in most major cities which can teach you and your management team the basics of HTML and get you to create a simple, flat web page in a day or so. While that won't gain you a second career as a coder, it will change the discussions you have about digital projects and give you a richer insight into which tasks are easy and which are hard.

2. Learn (a little) of structured query language (SQL). Your customer data is stored in a database, and questions are asked of that database using SQL. With a relatively small investment of time you can get your database team to show you what data is stored in your database and how they query the data to find out, say, all the customers who have not made a purchase recently and might need some marketing nudge. Again, that won't make you a database engineer, but it will prompt an interesting discussion about what kind of additional data you could gather about customers and sales transactions, and what that additional data might allow you to do.

3. Get (carefully) on to social media. These days you probably have a Twitter account and a Facebook page, but do you really use them? In any case, find out what other social media your customers use and make sure you are familiar with them too. Do they carry advertising? Is it possible to overhear discussions about your brand? Is this a viable way to make your management team more accessible to your customer?

4. More generally, make a practice of listening to customers talk about your brand online. Get good at searching on social media and elsewhere for discussions about your business and listen hard for both positive and negative stories. At least one giant of the New Normal got there by using each and every customer complaint as an opportunity to improve the end-to-end engineering of the business. You can't begin to do that unless you hear them in the first place.

5. Find a teenager and make them your mentor. One successful UK business identified bright young colleagues in stores and warehouses around the country and made sure that each senior

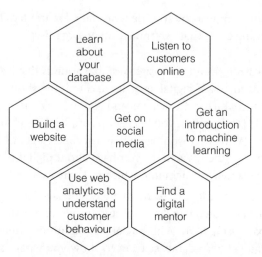

Figure 9.1 Seven digital learning goals

executive had a social media mentor who could talk to them about the digital world with the authority of a native.

6. Get familiar with how to track customer behaviour on your website. If your business uses Google Analytics, get someone to talk you through it and get a log-in of your own. Of course, some kind of aggregated reporting probably already exists in your business but looking in real time at customers actually searching and traversing your own site is incredibly rich information, akin to standing in a store and watching how customers shop.

7. Find a friendly trainer or data expert to give you a two-hour introduction to what machine learning is, how modern techniques can extract meaning from data and the kinds of business challenges which can be revolutionised by those approaches.

Back to the (digital) floor

Most retail and hospitality businesses will have some kind of 'back to the floor' programme to insist that at least once a year those colleagues who don't work in store go and spend some time there, ideally working several shifts to really experience customer interaction.

The reason they do that is obvious. People who are processing accounts, dealing with suppliers or building IT systems will inevitably do so better if they have a good understanding of what is happening at the front line as the business deals with its customers. When done well, these programmes can be transformative, not only educating back-office teams on customer challenges but also bringing the whole business together based on shared experiences.

The digital and data education programme we've highlighted here is really exactly the same thing. In the multi-channel world of the New Normal it is massively in everyone's interest to understand these new topics, and the process of learning about them together can be equally culturally significant.

> **I'd encourage you not just to make digital up-skilling a topic for your board or senior management team, but to find a way to take it right across the business.**

Not only will decisions at every level in the business be better for being more informed about the potential of digital channels and customer data, but as an added benefit you'll be delivering valuable skills and experiences to your colleagues. That's something that can't help but be good for engagement and retention.

Asking the right questions

There is one final aspect to getting match-fit, and that is to get really good at learning from other businesses. That might include others in your own industry that you can learn from by observation but also non-competing brands that are succeeding in the New Normal by doing things that you'd love to emulate in your own business.

That sounds like an obvious thing to do but happens surprisingly little, particularly among big businesses. I've had the good fortune to spend a lot of time working with small digital start-ups, not just in retail but in other sectors too. If there is one thing that separates the culture of Silicon Valley or London's Shoreditch digital businesses from more traditional retailers, it is their willingness to share with, and learn from, each other.

At organised networking events and in casual conversations in cities all around the world, start-ups are pooling their knowledge, connections and experiences in the deeply held belief that everyone succeeds together or no one succeeds at all. Even apparently competing businesses will often have good relationships with each other and share war stories of investments that have worked or failed.

That might all sound a bit too new age for you, and you might regard the idea of opening your heart to your nearest competitors with horror. But there is something to learn from the start-up culture, and that is not to be afraid to ask if you want to know something. I've seen leaders approach businesses in adjacent sectors to ask how they are getting such good results from a particular part of their business, and even seen whole management teams visit another business to try to experience the culture or decision-making approach that seems to be working so well. They have never been disappointed, and it is amazing how openly many businesses will share their perspectives and experiences with someone who just seems interested in what they have to say.

Bringing it together

An essential ingredient for the successful implementation of our strategy is that we gather some knowledge critical for the New Normal.

Even better, there is a double pay-off from doing that well, openly and in a way that engages all our colleagues. Not only is the business better off, but we get people excited about the new strategy and engaged in it right from the off.

And that becomes an important starting point as we'll see next. Most strategic change programmes fail. And most of them fail not because they are wrong, but because the organisation which needs to change rejects the idea, collectively shrugs its shoulders and carries on as it always has.

Now that we've articulated what we want to do to compete in the New Normal, set up the customer-focused KPIs which will track our progress and got ourselves fit for the journey, we need to face the next challenge. We need to build a strategic change programme which our people can really get behind and deliver, even as it challenges many of their long-held beliefs and hard-won skills. Getting things moving is the next challenge.

Chapter

10

Getting things moving

As the lights went down, there was a palpable buzz in the room.

As a young man with only a short stint in a management consultancy under my belt, I spent a few years working for a massive international technology company, with businesses operating in many countries on several continents. After a tough and slightly lacklustre few years of trading, the board of the business had assembled for an away day (or several) to work through a statement of the strategy for the business.

This was the strategy that would make sense of the slightly odd assortment of businesses around the world that made up the group, would articulate how the whole was going to be worth more than the sum of the parts, and would guide the business development activities of mortals like me for the next few years.

Several hundred folks from around the business had assembled in a great big hall near the head office and now the new strategy was going to be unveiled to us.

As green as I was, it took me longer than it should have to work out that the excitement I could feel all around me in the room was not based on anticipation of a new strategic direction for the business. Far from "I wonder what the future holds for us", the mood of the room was "I can't wait to see what rubbish these idiotic old men have come up with".

As if with one mind, the middle management of this grand company had folded their arms, sat back in their seats and rejected the strategy before the first speaker had even opened their mouth.

What made that even worse was that they were right. The strategy was a million miles from a clarion call to arms, and instead was a meandering justification of why the business was what it was already. Rather than guiding our future, it simply tried to rationalise our past.

Getting your strategy right

Two lessons stuck with me from that afternoon, and they are both relevant to our journey to reinvent retail.

The first is that the strategy for your business should be a good one. It should address your weaknesses, build on your strengths and represent a plan to build a defensible and sensible market position that allows you to generate a good return on investment based on great customer relationships. It should defend against your competitors and offer security and growth to your shareholders and your colleagues.

If you think that's obvious, you'd be surprised how much garbage I've seen in strategy presentations.

You should, however, have some great raw material for your reinvention strategy from the topics we've covered here. Understanding how your customers' needs have changed in the New Normal and working out how you can both build on your legacy strengths and also grow new revenue streams by doing business in different ways is a terrific starting point for strategy development.

Five questions to challenge your strategy with

By now, if you haven't done so already, you'll want to work with your management team to synthesise all that thinking into a pithy statement of what kind of business you are going to build, and what you will prioritise to do so.

As you do that, here are a set of five useful questions you can challenge the strategy with, to avoid looking as daft as the speakers above did:

1. Is the strategy recognisably building on who you are today? Remember the danger of creating a bullshit brand statement that is all wishful thinking and bears no relationship to reality. Your strategy needs to be one that your colleagues recognise as a journey that starts from where they are now.

2. Is the strategy clear? If you've had to define complicated words in order to express your desire to "bifurcate the market opportunity with value-added innovations" then you will not only lose your audience. You've probably also lost the clear central thought that would have allowed you to succeed. If you can't explain your strategy to a bright schoolkid or an elderly relative then it isn't clear enough.

3. Are you clear about your priorities? Try to do everything and you'll achieve little but focus the organisation on a small and manageable set of changes and you might get somewhere. I always challenge a newly formed strategy by asking 'if this is our strategy, what would we NOT do?' It's a surprisingly effective way of forcing a bit of focus.

4. If you are going to do new things (and in a reinvention strategy I hope you are), are you clear about how you are going to do that? Do you need new skills or technologies? Will you get them by hiring, or partnering, or acquiring other businesses?

5. Does your strategy make sensible assumptions about your competitors? If your five-year plan ignores the realities of the New Normal and assumes that Amazon will stop undercutting you on price, then it is a fairy story, not a strategy.

If you can answer those questions positively, you may very well have the core of a strategy that your people and other business stakeholders can buy into and get behind.

But the second lesson from my youthful experience with strategy presentations is a tougher challenge.

> **It is much, much harder to get people across your organisation to buy into your strategy than it is to write it down in the first place.**

There are several reasons why it is harder to get people across your organisation to buy into your strategy:

- **Your colleagues may not share with you the urgency of the need for change.** This is a particular challenge for many retailers where middle and senior management have been in retailing (and indeed with the same company) for a long time. They've seen recessions before and seen the business go through all sorts of other ups and downs. Rather than accepting that something significant and permanent has happened to create the New Normal, it is extremely tempting to simply assume that if they wait long enough, everything will fix itself and the world will go back to the way it used to be. That's an entirely understandable perspective and is also a dangerous one, because if we allow ourselves to think that way then we give ourselves an excuse to do nothing, which is usually most people's preferred course of action.

- Strategic change is also a significant **personal challenge** for many people in your organisation. As we've seen before, skills and experience which have taken years to gather can suddenly become less valuable. At the same time, new knowledge and skills are demanded by the New Normal, just when many of your middle and senior management have arrived at the stage of life where they are no longer comfortable learning new things. It's rare that this personal challenge is a conscious one. Most people are not that cynical and want to do the right thing for their organisation, but it is nonetheless often there and as a result it can be easier to get younger front-line colleagues excited about change than it is to get the middle layer of management to feel the same way.

- The third reason why your colleagues might be slow to buy into a reinvention strategy is that **they've been here before.** Most strategy presentations are, let's face it, vague and buzzwordy garbage. In that sense, it is no surprise that most people adopt an initial attitude of scepticism. This isn't their first rodeo.

- The final reason why your colleagues might be suspicious of the new strategy begins to point to how we might address this problem and get genuine buy-in. **If they weren't part of creating the strategy themselves,** they might be perfectly justified in feeling disenfranchised by the output. Indeed, observing a business which has just created and launched a new strategy initiative, you can usually tell who was at the meetings that created it just by observing body language. Those who were in the room feel excited, passionate and bought-in. Those who weren't, well, don't.

So our challenge is not only to come up with a great strategy to address the New Normal and secure the future of our business, but it is also to make sure that hundreds (or even thousands) of colleagues come to regard that strategy as their own, to feel it is mission-critical in the same way that we do, and therefore to become part of the effort to change the business. The alternative is passive resistance and inertia, and we don't have the time for that any more.

That's really difficult. Most strategies, however clever and well-articulated, fail to become the guiding mission for their organisation. Retail businesses have the toughest challenge of all in making this happen. Their business models are long-standing but hugely challenged in the New Normal, their middle management teams are often of long tenure with little experience of new channels to market and their front-line teams are physically dispersed around the world and consequently tricky to communicate with in an interactive way.

Daunting, isn't it? But this is the essential challenge of reinvention – finding a way to make a strategy into a way of life for an organisation.

The four steps to getting a strategy to stick

Here, building on years of observations of strategies that connect and strategies that don't, are four things that you and your leadership team can do to maximise your chance of success:

1. Co-create the strategy with your people.
2. Give the business a licence to change.
3. Keep it simple.
4. Celebrate.

Let's have a look at each tactic in turn.

Co-create the strategy with your people

If it's true that the people who were actually involved in creating your strategy are its most passionate advocates, then it stands to reason that you want as many people as possible involved in that process.

I've seen the two extremes of this. In one strategy creation process, we had cross-functional teams drawn from all parts of the business meet up for facilitated workshops that started by mapping out some realities of how our customers behaved and what our competitors were up to. We then moved on to discussing and prioritising options for what we could do about it all.

A gradual process brought all this work together and although a smaller central team ultimately decided on the priorities and produced the strategic summary, what came out was so recognisably built on the input from around the business that it was seen as the natural and inevitable conclusion of a process that the organisation collectively felt bought into.

At the other end of the scale, I've seen a new managing director of a business turn up to their first board meeting with a strategy sketched out on a single slide that they had presumably written on the train on the way in.

What struck me about the comparison was that at a purely academic level there wasn't much difference between the two strategies. The MD in the second example wasn't new to the business, understood its challenges well and did a pretty good job of articulating a three-pronged approach to the future. The longer and more inclusive process generated something similar.

But what was different, of course, was the reaction of the organisation. The MD with their one-pager had the experience of even their direct reports folding their arms and turning off. If the MD didn't care what they thought, why were they there? And if your strategy doesn't even have passionate buy-in from your board, you've got no chance with the wider organisation.

The more inclusive process has its disadvantages of course. It takes longer to get more people involved, costs money and there is the inevitable paradox for the CEO: if this comes up with something I don't like then I'm in trouble, and if it only comes up with things I like then why am I wasting my time with it?

But the reality is that engineering a cross-business strategy creation approach like this has benefits that vastly outweigh its costs:

- You can guide the process by carefully designing it and investing the time of your senior leaders to be in the conversations themselves.

- Conversely, there is always the danger that you'll learn something. Getting a broad cross-section of your people together in a room guarantees a range of customer and supplier perspectives that can really enhance a strategic plan.

- The inclusive process greatly helps to keep a strategy free of buzzwords and bullshit.

- By bringing together both head-office middle managers and people from your stores and distribution centres you can cut through some of the danger that the more senior people will reject the idea that change is needed. Real customer feedback is very persuasive.

- Going through the process creates advocates who will be incredibly useful later on. By carefully selecting people from around the business who are visible and are widely respected already, you give yourself the best possible chance of getting widespread buy-in later.

- Finally, there is a huge cultural benefit to building a strategy this way. You and your leadership team are seen to be involved and listening, you build communities of people around your business who might not otherwise even meet each other, and a well-moderated strategy day should be fun and inspiring. Not a bad way for your people to spend their time.

It's not, I don't think, too cynical to point out that you will rarely start a process like this with a blank sheet of paper. Just like the MD in our example, you'll usually have a fairly clear idea of where you want the business to go before you start, and I hope that working through this book has helped that process.

But even if you have an outcome in mind before you start, and carefully design your process to make sure that those themes are among the ones that get played back, the time invested in a co-creation process is worthwhile for all the reasons laid out above. Yes, you'll need to set a month or so aside to go through the process, but an organisation implementing a strategy that is owned and appreciated by its people will deliver so much faster than one which is having strategy 'done to it' that the time invested upfront will pay back handsomely.

Finally, a note about the organisation that ran the co-creation process I've described above. It saw big increases in customer satisfaction (NPS) and in market share over the following quarters, a direct result of the initiatives that came out of the process.

Give the business a licence to change

One business I worked with was particularly reluctant to try anything new. This was a long-established business and had had many years of what we'll politely call 'command and control leadership'. In other words, everyone was used to being told what to do and being yelled at when they did anything else.

I was trying to change the commercial strategy of the business to reverse a declining market share, but whenever I suggested something we might do I got the same answer: "We've tried that before" and "It doesn't work in our industry."

It took a little while before I stopped taking that at face value and started thinking about the organisational psychology that lay behind it. This was an organisation that didn't want to take risks and therefore wanted to avoid trying anything new or scary. The people in the business had had enough bad experiences with their leadership when things didn't work out that they had developed a coping strategy to avoid doing it again.

Now the thing was that when I suggested a particular pricing strategy or social media engagement idea I had no more than an educated hunch that they would work either. If they did then great, we'd make some money. And if they didn't, then we'd learn from that and move on to try something else. I wasn't trying to catch anyone out or make anyone look bad, but I did need the organisation to embrace the idea of trying new things, or else we'd never change our results.

Quite by accident, I hit on the magic form of words that allowed that to happen. I started to talk about a 'test and learn' strategy, where great innovative companies would try lots of things and would regard the failed experiments as just as valuable as the successful ones because they all contributed to improving the expertise of the business.

Fairly quickly, I started to hear the phrase being used by others in meetings and it rapidly became a buzz phrase across lots of different departments and countries. Then, under the umbrella of 'test and learn', people started to try things and report back on the results. Suddenly I didn't hear so much about how they'd tried that before and instead commercial meetings started to be filled with the things people had tested and the things they had learned.

There's nothing magic about the phrase 'test and learn', except that for that company at that time it changed the mindset. By reframing a failed experiment as a learning opportunity, it took the fear away from trying new things and the organisation turned out to have lots of great ideas up its sleeve – many of them better than the ones I was trying to suggest in the first place.

The magic phrase in your business might well be different, but the over-arching challenge is the same.

If you sense a degree of fear of trying new things, try to address it head on.

Your team might be worried about looking silly or damaging their careers or letting you down. Whatever the root cause, if your strategy requires your business to experiment with a myriad of new ideas and tactics, try to create an environment where trying new things is celebrated as an end in itself.

Giving the organisation permission to experiment like this has another hidden pay-off. In the last chapter we talked about getting the organisation match-fit by encouraging your colleagues to develop new skills for the New Normal. Often the barriers to self-development are similar to the barriers to trying new strategies. No one wants to look silly or suggest that they weren't up to speed already and so it can be surprisingly tough to get colleagues (especially long-standing ones) to learn new things.

Giving your people, as well as the organisation at large, the sense that this is a business which welcomes innovation and celebrates new skills can unlock a flood of investment in learning and development that can turbo-charge your reinvention.

Keep it simple

Several times we've seen that the key drivers of an increased NPS score are often very straightforward. Welcoming customers into store in a warm and personable way, having a clean and tidy store, having clean toilets in a cinema – these are the mainstays of operational execution and make more difference to customers than how many segments you have in your email model.

As we explored in Rule 4, the power of a greeting in a store is more subtle than it first seems. It isn't the action of saying hello that matters (otherwise those awful parroted corporate greetings would actually work). It is the sub-text that matters. Someone in the store cares that you are there and is therefore on hand to deal with any questions, complaints or other needs that you might have. By engaging with customers in this way we make them feel welcome, which is not a bad way to start a relationship.

So quite a sophisticated aspect of customer engagement strategy can be boiled down to 'just say hello'. And in the same way, other aspects of our strategy can be given simple headlines as well:

- Give the same experience in store and online.
- Charge the right price to make every sale.
- Treat every interaction with a customer as part of an ongoing relationship.
- Never leave a complaint unresolved.
- Put a smile on every face.

All easy to say, but potentially representing quite subtle and far-reaching strategies with implications for our commercial policies, human resources policies and much more.

There's real power in having some simple and memorable statements that sum up aspects of your strategy. The transmission of the message from one person to another is faster for one. They also serve as valuable talismans when someone needs to work out what to do in a new or unexpected situation. If the number one objective of the strategy is 'build the customer relationship', then it becomes straightforward to figure out what to do with a complaint or when a delivery goes missing.

Of course, there is a danger too.

> **Organisations, and particularly multi-site businesses like retail, have an unnerving ability to take things literally.**

Our 'say hello to the customer' example illustrates this well. I'm sure you can imagine the kind of organisation that would take a thought like that and turn it into a soulless but mandatory script and then measure compliance with the strategy via a mystery shopping programme.

Even if yours is a business which would not do something so simplistic, you'll need to take care that that kind of 'literal compliance' approach doesn't pop up in one region or even in individual stores.

But in the end, a strategy which can be summarised in simple phrases is an effective one. Your effort in communicating the strategy can then be focussed on bringing those phrases to life with stories that show the subtlety and the underlying meaning of the phrase, making sure that your organisation at large is fully empowered to bring the strategy to life.

Celebrate

My fourth tip for bringing your strategy to life around the organisation is another one that sounds obvious but happens all too rarely. As you start to see the first shoots of strategy implementation around the business, you have a great opportunity to reinforce the change by first noticing it and then celebrating it.

At first, you'll be celebrating that the strategy is happening at all. You'll get a letter from a customer who was treated particularly well or a trade journal will notice your new more sophisticated pricing strategy.

Eventually, of course, what you'll want to celebrate will be the results from the strategy too. Market share rising, customers returning, sales rising, NPS going up – all are things you can use to build confidence and momentum around the business.

Don't underestimate how frequently and loudly this type of communication needs to happen.

> **Within reason, an organisation which is undergoing major strategic change needs to see a positive message about the change and its results at least every week, and you need to use a variety of communications media to achieve that.**

I've seen organisations use email and newsletters, but also seen very effective use of short video messages from senior leaders sent to desktops or mobile devices.

Apart from frequency, the other key success factor for this type of communication is authenticity. I worked for an interesting CEO once who decided during a major and difficult change programme that he was going to personally author a 'what happened this week' email to every employee. He was honest even when delivering tough messages and the impact was powerful. Even long-standing and quite cynical employees would acknowledge that they knew what was going on and why, and respected the leadership of the business for communicating in the way they did.

His successor, however, undid all that good. He didn't want to write a weekly email like that, but because of the precedent his predecessor had set he couldn't stop either. Instead, he delegated it to the PR department who sent out a dull email listing all the new corporate clients signed up that week. That did neither morale nor the CEO's reputation any good.

Bringing it together

If you thought that coming up with a strategy to cope with the New Normal was tricky, getting it to stick across the organisation turns out to be trickier still.

Take the time, and make the investment, however, in 'landing' the strategy with the organisation using the tools we've laid out here and you will maximise your chances of making reinvention into a movement with real energy and momentum.

And that's just as well, because even once you've done that you've only won over one constituency. In the real world of reinventing retail there are several more you need to convince, including those pesky shareholders. That's what we'll turn our attention to next.

Chapter

11

Taking people with you

It's always worth reading the small print. Sometimes it even ends up being helpful.

When you become a director of a company, one particularly relevant chunk of small print is the company law that sets out your responsibilities and your legal obligations. In the UK, this is governed by the 2006 Companies Act and in the US and other territories there are equivalent frameworks.

When I first became a director, I was lucky enough to have someone who took the time to talk me through the obligations I was taking on, and I'm glad they did because I learned something new.

I knew enough about business that I was certain that my responsibility as a director was to maximise the value of the business for its shareholders, right? Wrong. The UK law, and that of many US states, makes clear that the responsibility of a company director is to a much broader set of stakeholders in the business, not just to the shareholders.

That set of stakeholders is rarely defined precisely, but can be taken to include the following groups:

- the employees of the business and former employees
- your customers
- your suppliers and other business partners and creditors
- the communities and environments within which your business operates
- the government, regulators and other public bodies
- your shareholders, lenders and other financial stakeholders.

That's a comprehensive list, and one which is open to interpretation, argument and even legal challenge. In a famous US example from 1919, shareholders in Ford Motor Company sued Henry Ford because he had the nerve to say that he wanted the benefits of the company's success to be spread around customers and employees as well as stockholders. (They won, but in one of those cases that ended up changing the law even further.)

For retailers, this list of stakeholders is especially important, and it is a terrible mistake to think of it as the template for a set of words to be grudgingly referenced in some dull annual report text to satisfy the law.

Why is this broader list of stakeholders so important to us?

> **Stakeholders are important because any one of them can thwart our newly minted strategy for the New Normal, and indeed it takes the support and willing cooperation of a broad range of these interest groups to really make a new strategy stick.**

Building a coalition for change

Here then is our final challenge in building and implementing a strategy to reinvent our business. We've worked out our plan and built a motivated and engaged team around the business who are empowered to make the change. We are clear about what we need to do that's new, what we need to do to make the best use of our historic strengths, and we have set up KPIs that will allow us to track progress, celebrate and accelerate.

But in just the same way that it can be difficult to get colleagues around the business bought into the need to change the business, it can be difficult to get other groups of stakeholders engaged too, and often for similar reasons.

Different stakeholder groups will have a direct financial interest in our business that might seem to be challenged by a reinvention strategy:

- If our journey means reducing the number of stores we operate, then there are obvious consequences for those invested in those stores. That most directly impacts our own colleagues who work there but will also draw the attention of the landlords who will lose a tenant, the local authority or town centre manager who will be worried about the impact of a void on other retailers, as well as customers who may have used that store for years and be attached to it.

- If we are changing the way we do business with customers (moving to online selling, for instance, or repositioning stores as part of a multi-channel experience), then that will clearly impact many of our employees and will also involve unions, trade associations, suppliers and others.

- Changes to where we employ people again can have knock-on impacts, attracting concern from local press, MPs and councillors for affected areas and local community groups.

Other potential objections to watch out for

Beyond the purely financial, there are all sorts of other reasons why different stakeholder groups might find a new strategy challenging or difficult to support. Some are simply emotional. Change can be scary to many people for the same reasons that it can be within the business. People can worry that they might need new skills or do things in new ways and most of us would rather do things the way we always have, given half a chance.

Some objections to change are also political, with either a small or a large 'p'. It might suit some stakeholders to object to change or to campaign for things to go back to the way they once were for reasons that have little to do with our specific business but are more about signalling a wider point about society or government.

This can be the case with technology change which has often been opposed by interest groups worried that the specific community or skillset that they represent will become marginalised. Many industries that have been through significant changes to computerised technologies have had to fight long battles with multiple stakeholder groups to get there, with the introduction of digital printing in the newspaper industry a particularly graphic example.

Changes in working practices can suffer from the same thing. A good example from recent years has been the growth in the gig economy and short hours contracts that offer greater flexibility but much less certainty to both employers and employees. There is indeed still much to learn about the best role for this type of employment practice and for how the more flexible workforce they create can be achieved in ways that also deliver dignity and financial security to employees. But the political battles on the subject in recent years have often been more about throwing rocks than finding answers.

The all-important shareholders

And then, standing astride over all these stakeholder groups with their different and competing needs are your shareholders. While they might only be one group of stakeholders, they are a very important one for some obvious reasons.

I've been privileged to sit on the boards of businesses of multiple types. Public companies, with their thousands of shareholders, onerous transparency requirements and boards of elected directors, but also privately owned businesses with either a private equity fund or one or more individuals and families as their ultimate owners.

There are certainly differences between these environments. But they are also united in one key way. Collectively, the shareholders of the business have the most obvious and direct financial stake in the success of the company and will take a correspondingly direct interest in its fortunes. They also, one way or another, hire and fire the management of the business which is something else we'll want to keep in mind!

How best, then, can we wrangle all these important stakeholders and make them supporters and drivers of our reinvention rather than critics and barriers? That's not easy, particularly when the change is likely to be costly and painful, but here are four tips you might consider to help along the way.

The stakeholder wheel

The mistake I observe most CEOs make when promoting a change programme is to get too mesmerised by one stakeholder group and pay too little attention to the others.

The most precious commodity any executive has is their own time. There is always far too much to do in any business, and it seems perfectly logical that the first priority of all should be actually doing the job. It feels much better to most business leaders to be reviewing trading, visiting stores, talking to suppliers or making decisions in meetings rather than lunching with a non-executive director or talking to the local MP.

As we've seen, however, almost any group of your stakeholders has the power to either help or hinder the reinvention of your business, and so you will need an active plan to connect with each of them, explaining your plan and managing their concerns.

My suggestion is that you use the stakeholder wheel, an example of which you can see below. The first step is to create the wheel by considering all the constituencies you regard as important for this exercise. That will vary from business to business – in some, unions are important and in others not. It will also vary from country to country – in many European territories the employee works council is far too important to be ignored.

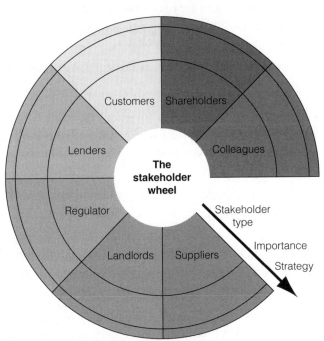

Figure 11.1 The stakeholder wheel

The second ring of the wheel asks you and your team to consider how important each of those groups is to the task in front of you. Some will be absolutely mission-critical, controlling budget approval for key planning and property decisions. Others might be potentially noisy and vocal, but not actually have quite so much impact on the outcome of your plan.

The third ring requires us to think about our actual strategy for each group of stakeholders. Now I'm cheating a bit, because the strategies themselves won't really fit on the wheel, but it is worth going deliberately through the exercise of thinking about the right way to approach each group. To do that, you might consider the following:

- What that stakeholder group thinks of your business right now.
- What concerns, or indeed opportunities, they might see in your proposed reinvention plan,
- What they need to hear, and what evidence they need to see, to be convinced that you are right in your proposals.
- What, if any, horse-trading might be possible. Is there some give-and-take that might secure their support?
- What evidence will they use to evaluate if you are making progress or not?

You can, if you wish, add a final, outside ring of the strategy to allow you as a team to consider who is going to own the engagement with each stakeholder group, even if they need to bring others in from time to time.

Thinking about your stakeholder engagement in this way achieves three important things.

First, it makes your engagement with these groups a deliberate and strategic act rather than a haphazard or occasional one. Whatever difficulties you might have in keeping everyone on side, the whole thing will be easier if you go into the process with a plan.

Second, it allows you to build the plan as a leadership team, together. If your own time is your most precious commodity, then it makes sense to allocate tasks across the group and to use the talents, contacts and resources of as many people as possible to create momentum.

Finally, it makes the plan a dynamic one. I've seen teams review the stakeholder wheel every week, just to keep up with what's going on and make sure that the right progress is being made. Conversely, the first time I ever drew up a version of the wheel for myself, the first thing I did was put it in a drawer and realise only a few weeks later that I had left a couple of key groups under-contacted, something which indeed became exactly the problem for our change programme that you would expect. So don't just build the wheel – use it.

Consider both 'towards' and 'away from' influencing

As with any negotiation, getting a stakeholder group on board will require a whole range of influencing strategies. Some groups will want to know that others are on board. (A deliberate use of PR can be invaluable in helping you achieve that sense that 'everyone else is with us'.)

One big distinction in influencing strategies where I've seen teams come unstuck, though, is that between 'towards' and 'away from'. Ask someone why they changed jobs last, and the type of explanation you'll hear varies a bit depending on the person. Some will immediately begin by articulating what attracted them about the job they are doing now. Others will focus more on the reasons why they left the previous role. In the first case, the person is articulating what drew them <u>towards</u> the next job, while in the second they are talking about what pushed them <u>away from</u> the old job.

In practice, most people will use a blend of these explanations to justify their decision. Indeed, it can be quite difficult sometimes to tell them apart. "I moved jobs because the new one offered me leadership experience" sounds positive, but on careful listening can be a disguised way of saying "My old job didn't offer me leadership experience."

However complex it might be, though, the distinction between towards and away from motivations is a helpful filter to apply when engaging with your stakeholder groups. If, for example, your board of directors is fundamentally concerned about change and worried about taking what it sees as the risk of reinventing the business, then you might find that no number of presentations about how great the future will be once the plan succeeds will work. They'll listen, of course, but it will feel like the strategy is just not quite connecting.

The thing to try in that situation is to switch from towards to away from and begin to articulate what might happen to the business if you don't change. Market share lost to new competitors, margins eroded, brand leadership disappearing. All are powerful potential motivators for the 'away' from stakeholder.

The opposite is also true. For some people, no amount of "We are doomed if we don't change" will work. They need to be sold on a vision of where the strategy is taking them.

So by listening and observing carefully, and ensuring that your influencing messages are the right blend of towards and away, you maximise your chances of getting everyone on board.

Remember the sunk cost fallacy

We've met the sunk cost fallacy already as it applies to ourselves and our teams, but if anything it is an even bigger danger for other stakeholder groups, and perhaps biggest of all for your shareholders and the analysts and financial journalists who present your story to them. After all, it is your shareholders who have borne the costs of your existing business.

If there is a common thread to the dozens and dozens of retail business failures we've seen over the last decade it is probably denial. Denial that change is needed, denial that new competitors might become market leaders in their own right, denial that changing consumer habits and the other realities of the New Normal require a totally different approach to business.

That's entirely understandable. As we've seen several times already, people have built careers, reputations, incomes and status on their knowledge of how things are, and their ability to thrive in a particular business climate. As that climate changes, there is a danger that those investments in personal skills, networks and knowledge become less valuable than they were. And that is a terrifying prospect.

As true as that is for the emotional and personal capital of your people, it is also true for the investments (financial and otherwise) made in your business by the stakeholder groups we are talking about here.

So how can we make it easier to sell into our stakeholders a strategy that means discarding or writing off assets which were once important but are now sunk? The best approach is honestly, respectfully, pragmatically and creatively:

- **Honestly** in the sense that there is no point pretending that something painful isn't true. Let's imagine that in your reinvention strategy you need far fewer stores, or that you need to rebuild a distribution and logistics platform that you only installed fairly recently. These are classic sunk costs and it is important to highlight them right alongside the opportunities that you are chasing with your strategy.

- **Respectfully** in the sense that it is important to acknowledge that the cost that you are choosing to regard as sunk is still a painful one. In our store closure example people's livelihoods will be lost. In our distribution and logistics example there will be people around the table who were involved in signing off the systems that you now want to replace. You might even be one of them yourself. There is no value in being flippant about the costs of your reinvention strategy, but at the same time there is no point using the fact that they might be embarrassing to ignore them.

- **Pragmatically and creatively** because there is much more to a sunk cost than just a line in a presentation. There may be clever ways to re-use assets in other parts of your business or indeed to sell them to others who can make better use of them. There will certainly be a whole range of ways to approach writing off a sunk cost. The rise of the CVA in the UK in recent years represents one way retailers have approached reducing the size of their store estates in (more or less) partnership with landlords, and others will emerge too.

As we've seen already, it is critical that we approach our strategy of reinvention with a clear view about which of our historical assets is going to help us on our journey. It is equally critical, however, that we are clear about which parts of our businesses are not going to help. That's always the toughest message for stakeholders to come to terms with, but it is an important hurdle to cross.

Build momentum

Finally, your stakeholders will need evidence, just like your own team will, if they are to stick out the journey. There is a rational reason for that, of course. No reinvention strategy is risk-free and your stakeholders will need reasons to believe that they haven't made a terrible mistake backing your plan (or backing you).

But there is also an emotional reason why early evidence is so important. If you've painted a clear picture of where the business is going and provided the right mix of towards and away from reasons why people should support that change, then you will have created two powerful emotions among your own people and your wider stakeholder group – excitement and fear.

Excitement because everyone wants to be involved in a successful change, and the chances are that by the time you have created your plan it will be intuitively clear to many that the status quo was not going to cut it.

Fear, though, because very few change plans work and no one wants to back a dud.

When you begin to see early evidence of momentum, the combination of relief and enthusiasm that is unlocked from that mix of fear and excitement can be very powerful. Not only will it win you support for the next phase of the plan, but you may also find that people want to get more involved, share ideas of their own and actively help the business get further on its journey.

> *By taking steps to find, share and celebrate early evidence of success, you can effectively widen your team and deepen its support, something that can deliver a step-change in momentum all on its own.*

Bringing it together

We first started building our reinvention plan in Part 1 by looking outwards – at changes in the world, at the evolving needs of our customers and at those pesky new entrants into our markets.

We've then spent the bulk of Part 2 looking inwards – at our business, our people, our systems and even at ourselves and our skills and knowledge.

It is fitting, then, that in this critical final chapter of Part 2 we've begun to look out again at the stakeholders who have invested, financially and in other ways, in building the business we have today and who are vital constituencies as we consider the business we want to become.

By considering each of those constituencies deliberately, building an engagement plan for each one and being direct, honest and respectful with them, we can begin to build a coalition for our reinvention. At first that might be a set of stakeholders who have at least given their permission for our plan, but as we build and share momentum it can and should become a set of stakeholders who are actively involved themselves and regard our success as their own.

That's not to say there aren't difficult conversations to be had. There are bound to be sets of stakeholders who lose out from change, particularly as we use physical stores differently or shift technologies. But the consequences of us not trying to change at all are likely to be worse, even for them, and so it ought to be possible to win them over.

We've come a long way over the course of this book and covered a lot of ground. Let's take a moment to look back at where we started and the journey we've been on.

In conclusion

In the Introduction to this book I described the experience of stumbling out into the night after a long meeting trying to save a retailer that had not embraced change quickly enough – an experience sadly shared by many other leadership teams in recent years.

Under that pressure, there is a natural tendency to look for causes outside our own businesses. Indeed, the New Normal presents challenges for society and government as well as for business leaders. Inflexible property contracts; the business rates paid by retailers but not really paid by internet start-ups; the clever tax 'minimising' that an international business without stores can get up to. All of these are topics worth time and discussion if we are to rebuild retailing.

But none of that is enough. Making business, commercial and financial life easier for retailers will help, for sure, but it isn't in itself the change that the New Normal demands.

That's where we come in. By understanding the implications of the New Normal for our customers, and therefore for our own businesses, we can begin to make a plan not just to recover but to rebuild. We will do that by engaging our colleagues across the business, bringing new knowledge and technology into the organisation, surrounding ourselves with customer-facing and change-oriented KPIs and then unleashing the passion and energy of our people towards a clearly articulated strategy.

I hope that *Reinventing Retail* has helped you on your quest to do that. By thinking differently about your brand, your pricing strategy, your customer communications and the ways you enable your colleagues to inspire your customers, you will create the next chapter of the story for your business.

This book is not, and could never be, a step-by-step 'cut out and keep' guide that you simply follow page by page. Instead, its purpose has been to provide inspiration and food for thought – essential ingredients to allow you and your team to form a strategy ideal for your own business and your own market.

In particular, as you worked through Part 1, I hope you took note of the action planning sections. Each of them represents a window into a topic that could play an important role in your strategy creation. They are all drawn from real strategy projects that I have worked on in one business or another and, while they may not all be relevant to every business, I am confident that at least some of them will be worth you spending quality time working through.

The strategy that results from working through Part 1 might require you to shrink or otherwise drastically change your store estate. It will certainly force you to think through from first principles why you have stores in the New Normal and the value you can deliver there for your customers.

Equally, the strategy development process should make you think differently about your digital presence. Is a vanilla website that lists products and has a checkout enough, or do you need to provide content and inspiration alongside your product listings? Are you making the right use of social media and other richer ways of connecting with customers?

And Part 1 of this book should also have encouraged you to think differently about your customers themselves. How have their needs changed? How do they see your product category and your brand? Indeed, how do you know that? What methods can you use to stay connected to genuine customer feedback and experience? What do you know about your customers and how are you putting customer data to work to out-manoeuvre your competitors?

All of these and more can be ingredients of a reinvention programme. Every price point, every customer contact, every opportunity to make a sale or win-back a dissatisfied customer will matter more than ever in the New Normal. If nothing else is true about the world today, it is true that customers have more choice.

That can be a lot to deal with, and the plan you create for your business may well involve bold, difficult and costly changes. That's why Part 2 of the book is so important – lifting your plan off the page and making it happen will be the biggest challenge of all, and you'll need every trick in the leadership book to get there. I hope some of the suggested approaches and tips in Part 2 will help you achieve that. Just like the action planning exercises in Part 1, all the suggestions in Part 2 are for approaches which I have either done myself or seen at first hand, and they can really make a difference to changing your business.

It falls to those of us who lead, advise and invest in retail businesses to step up to the challenges presented by the New Normal and take retail businesses, many of them with business practices decades old, and get them ready to grow and thrive for decades to come.

In that great venture, I wish you well. When you stumble out onto a street at 2am wondering how to get home, I hope it is because you have been celebrating success with your team, winning awards and recognition for the way your business has reinvented itself, taken on the internet giants and built valuable customer relationships along the way. I'll be cheering you on.

Index

Page numbers followed by *f* indicate figures

active selling 89
actively listening to customers 51
AirBnB 119, 124
Allen, Woody 80
Amazon 9, 89, 135
Apple 94, 100–1
authenticity 66–70, 188

'back to the floor' programme 172–3
brand 14
  and authenticity 66–70
  development 65
  experiencing 101
  values 63–4
brand reputation online 59–62
  building 65
  risks 73–4
bundles/bundling
  kinds of 122–3
  reasons for buying 120–1
business
  with bad memories 102–4
  changing commercial strategy
    of 184
  competitive advantage 37
  measure of market share in 7
  online 108–11
  reputation 57–75
  right strategy for 85
business change programme 159

change(s)
  building coalition for 192–3
  objections to 193
  in technology xv
Cialdini, Robert 22
co-creation of strategy 181–4

command and control leadership 184
Companies Act (2006) 191
competitive/comparative advantage
  35, 37–8
consumers
  response to incentives 105
  valuing experiences/products 24–5
convenience 88
cost sunk fallacy 139*f*
curation 88
'customer closeness' programme
  153, 155
customer lifetime value (CLV)
  concept of 48–9
  maths of 48*f*
  for online businesses 109*f*
  revisited 111
customers
  engaging with 186
  feedback 51–2, 66
  identifying pain-points 43
  key to profiting from 44–6
  listening to 51, 65
  online 112
  personalising products and services
    for 25–8
  power of data 106–8
  profitability of individual 29
  relationships 99–114
  reviewing individual
    complaints 158
  service, experiencing 158
  using web analytics to understand
    behaviour 172
  valuable 103
customisation/personalisation, of
  products 25–8, 30

data, customer 106–8
digital mentor, finding 171–2
digital skills
    action plan for learning 170–2
    asking the right questions 173–4
    'back to the floor' programme 172–3
    building 165–74
    investment, in technology 166–7
    technology terms 168–70
direct effects of technology change xv
dis-intermediation 117–26
discount 105, 122
    rate 49
discovery 88
distribution strategy 81–2
    in New Normal 85–90
Dollar Shave Club 107
'drivers' model, building 154
Duoboots 27

e-commerce xvi, 28
engagement 149
excitement and fear 200
experiences, unlocking power
        of 24–5, 30

Facebook 137
fear and excitement 200
feedback, gathering
    from customer 51–2, 66
first-order impacts, of technology
        change xv
Ford, Henry 192
4 Ps 80
four-stage strategy process 141–3

Games Workshop 94
Goodhart, Charles 150

hello, power of 154–5
HMV 70
holiday package market 117–19, 123
Hotel Chocolat 19, 94, 121

iMacs 100
immediacy and scarcity 15–17, 30
incentives 105
Influence (book by Cialdini) 22
information, sharing of 40
innovation 36
    ideas, mapping 21f
    and product differentiation 19–21
internet, arrival of 39–40
investment, in technology 166–7
iPhone 89, 100

Jobs, Steve 100

Keynes, John Maynard 49
knowing your customers 99–114
knowledge, access to 39–44

learning, action plan for digital 170–2
linked sales 88–9
listening, power of 50–3, 65
location strategy, challenge of 79–96
low-price new entrants, five critical
        strategies to compete with 12–28
    consumers valuing experiences as
        well as products 24–5
    immediacy and scarcity 15–17
    innovation and product
        differentiation 19–21
    personalising products and services
        for customers 25–8
    use wisdom of crowd to get
        customers 22–4
low-profit competition 5–6
loyalty card paradox 104–6, 112
Lush 66–7, 93–4

machine learning 107, 172
market share, analysis of 7–9, 160
merchandising 122

Nectar programme 104
net promoter score (NPS) 149–50

equation 150*f*
five key steps to using 155–6
Goodhart's Law and 151
improving score 152–3
and KPI 160–1
and market share 160–1
and New Normal 156–7
reasons for 150
using to drive real change 158–60
Netflix 63, 91
New Normal xvi–xviii
    four-stage strategy process 141–3
    net promoter score (NPS) and 156–7
    rule 1: entrants to sell your products
        at cost or less 5–32
    rule 2: everyone knows
        everything 35–53
    rule 3: reputation will make or
        break a business 57–75
    rule 4: location matters 79–96
    rule 5: knowing your customer
        99–114
    rule 6: strange pic-n-mix world of
        dis-intermediation 117–26

online brand reputation 58–62

'people who bought this product also
        bought that one' approach 89
personalisation, of products and
        services 25–8, 30
place
    in New Normal 81–3
    power of 80–1
plan, building 133–46
politics, cautionary lesson from 62
price-based competition 6
pricing
    comparison 6
    factors affecting 18*f*
    strategy 18–19, 53
Primark 10
product experience 88

product innovation/differentiation,
        finding opportunities for
        19–21, 30

reputations
    online 57–75
    people making 70–3
retail and data challenge 112–13
retailers, new world for xiv–xv
reviews, impacting reputation 58–62
rewards 105
risk taking 73–4
Ryanair 67

scarcity and immediacy 15–17, 30
second-order impacts, of technology
        change xv, xvii
shareholders 194
Simpson, Homer 12
social media, get on 171
stakeholders 191–2
    wheel 194–7, 195*f*
store, role of 88
strategy
    of business, changing 184–5
    celebration 187–8
    co-creation process 181–4
    customer engagement
        strategy 186–7
    five questions to challenge 178–81
    four-stage process 141–3
    four steps to getting 181–8
    getting right 178
    influencing 197
structured query language (SQL) 171
subscription 123
Sun Tzu 86
sunk cost fallacy 138–40, 198–200
survival xix–xx

technology
    changes in xv
    investments in 166–7

Tesco Clubcard 104
'test and learn' strategy 184–5
Timpsons 94
'towards' and 'away from'
    motivations 197–8
Toys R Us 94–5
transaction costs 40, 80–1, 83
TripAdvisor 23, 57
Twitter 40, 137

Uber 119, 120, 124
un-bundling 119–20
  risk 121

video streaming business 136

Wagamama 20
website, learning to build 171
WH Smith 16, 79, 85
WiFi service 112–13

Yelp 57

'zero-based' and bold approach 91